YOUR COMEBACK

TONY EVANS

HARVEST HOUSE PUBLISHERS
EUGENE, OREGON

Cover design by Byrce Williamson

Cover Image © Lauren Guy Photography

Some material previously published in *The Perfect Christian* by Tony Evans, copyright © 1999 by Tony Evans. Used by permission of Thomas Nelson. www.thomasnelson.com

YOUR COMEBACK
Copyright © 2018 by Tony Evans
Published by Harvest House Publishers
Eugene, Oregon 97408
www.harvesthousepublishers.com

ISBN 978-0-7369-6064-9 (pbk.)
ISBN 978-0-7369-6065-6 (eBook)

Library of Congress Cataloging-in-Publication Data is on file at the Library of Congress, Washington, DC.

Printed in the United States of America

18 19 20 21 22 23 24 25 26 / VP-CD / 10 9 8 7 6 5 4 3 2 1

CONTENTS

MY OWN COMEBACK

If there is one thing you can count on in your life, it's that your path will not always be easy.

It happens to all of us sometimes. Everything seems to be going well for you, and then suddenly a turn of events brings discouragement and frustration, and you feel like you just want to give up. Maybe you've racked up so many bad decisions that you've almost put any kind of happiness out of reach. You might feel as though you are at the end of your rope, just hanging on for dear life. Or it seems like after a good start you are now running dead last in the race of life, and the finish line looks so far away that you might wonder if you can make it at all.

Our lives are filled with setbacks—those times when things just aren't going our way, when victory seems out of our grasp, when happiness and contentment seem downright impossible. Occasional setbacks are probably unavoidable—part of the struggle of living in a fallen world. Other setbacks are due to our own sin and failures, or circumstances outside out control. But God has an answer for our every setback; He wants to orchestrate a *comeback* in our lives.

I know because I've been there. I can relate.

It's a miracle that I am where I am today. Let me tell you something I don't talk about very often. Maybe you'll find it encouraging.

When I was younger, I had a terrible problem with stuttering. It was hard to get through a sentence without hesitation and a bunch of distracting little fillers, like "…umm…" and "…er…" For years, just getting a complete sentence out of my mouth on the first try was nearly impossible.

Soon after my conversion I knew I wanted to be a speaker who would share about Christ to a room full of listeners. But who would have the patience to listen through all my stuttering? My parents and doctors didn't know why I stuttered, and they didn't know how to help me. I couldn't express my thoughts clearly, and it looked like I might have to give up my dreams of becoming a speaker.

But God, in His wisdom, had chosen to use me—even as a broken mouthpiece for Him. I wouldn't give up even though the circumstances were lined up against me. I was tempted to let go of my dream, but instead I held on to God. My comeback didn't happen overnight. I had to work, I had to practice, I had to pray, and I had to get some help from trained speech therapists.

And God gave me a comeback. Today I speak in front of

people all the time. Every Sunday I preach two sermons, each nearly an hour in length, to thousands of people. And I regularly travel around the country to speak to large gatherings of people. I've spoken in front of crowds as large as a million people. I never hesitate to say yes to an opportunity to share my faith in front of an audience. Me, the kid who couldn't speak a single sentence with clarity or confidence due to my stuttering. Some would have counted me out, but God never did. And I never gave up because it wasn't easy.

I could tell you a lot of other stories about how God has provided comebacks in my life, such as when it seemed academically and financially impossible for me to go to seminary. None of the circumstances were in my favor, and I was sometimes tempted to quit trying. I didn't have the money and I didn't have the grades. And the school I wanted to attend was one that rarely admitted African-Americans at that time. It would have been easy to give up and lower my goals. But God provided a comeback. Though I was only accepted on probation, I worked hard, and with God's help I turned around my academic record. I eventually graduated with honors and became the first African-American to graduate from Dallas Theological Seminary with an earned doctoral degree.

Now, with God's deliciously ironic way of doing things, I am overseeing a worldwide media ministry and online training center for pastors and lay leaders. Part of enjoying my own comeback is helping make one available for others. The Tony Evans Training Center offers high quality courses in Bible, theology, and Christian living with the goal of developing kingdom disciples (tonyevanstraining.org).

Comebacks don't seem likely when your back is up against the wall and your hope is depleted. But if you will stay the course, you will discover God's power to reverse the irreversible in your life. It is my hope that the principles and truths in these pages will equip you with the mindset you need to experience the comeback you need. God is the God of second and third—and fourth chances. He can turn things around on a dime. Look to Him always, honor Him first, and then watch Him blow your mind.

Remember, our God can hit a bulls-eye with a crooked stick.

Part 1
EXAMPLES OF COMEBACKS

1

THINK DIFFERENT

Apple hasn't always been the dominating tech company it is today, wrapping its brand around the world and penetrating diverse cultures. This innovation leader hasn't always been able to expect customers to stand in line for days before the release of a new product, sleeping in blankets on sidewalks just to secure that coveted first buy.

At one time, the media predicted Apple was destined for failure. They also assaulted its eccentric leader, Steve Jobs, with critical review after critical review. Those who followed stock advisers' sound advice to buy low and sell high could have bought plenty of low-priced Apple stock at one time.

In 1997, the future looked bleak for this unique computer company that targeted creative users rather than the typical upper-class demographic. IBM owned the general market and shaped the mindset for the computer savvy at the time. IBM's watchword, "THINK," had been rolled out in million-dollar campaigns aimed at capturing the entire market for personal gadgets. In 1999, IBM would roll out yet another campaign, this time expanding its aim to small businesses with the tagline, "Solutions for a small planet." Yet the price tag of that campaign wasn't small, costing IBM more than $40 million when all was said and done.[1]

But by then, it would be too late.

In 1998, Apple introduced the iMac. But many observers agree that it wasn't primarily this revolutionary new product that transformed Apple's reputation. Instead, IBM fell from premiere to paltry in many consumers' minds because the previous year, Apple challenged the world to do more than "THINK." Rather, they challenged each of us to "Think different."

But how was this new? After all, Apple had always been different. Its history and founders were considered rebellious, arrogant, and ostentatious. That branding style had proven to be a negative in the past, so why would "thinking different" be so appealing now?

"Different" succeeded this time because some clever marketing minds helped us all to see "different" in a new light. They did this by couching "different" in the context of world-changing history. The campaign's leader described his idea this way:

> Martin Luther King was seen as a troublemaker before he was universally seen as a saint, the rebellious Ted Turner was laughed out of town when he first tried to sell the concept of a 24-hour news channel, and it's been said that before Einstein was celebrated as the world's greatest thinker, he was thought to be just a guy with crazy ideas. Of course in 1997, Apple was being called a "toy" that was only for "creative types," and it was being chastised for not having the same operating

system as everyone else. But I felt this copy would speak to the fans and get people who weren't on our side to re-evaluate their thinking and realize that being different is a good thing.[2]

The "Think different" campaign creators had to think different just to get their oddball idea backed by Steve Jobs himself. Those in the inner circle later revealed that Jobs didn't even want to do TV ads when he first reached out to marketing agencies to somehow dig Apple out of its hole in 1997. But this agency managed to change his mind with their pitch. They told him they would script the ad based on the feel and energy of the popular film *Dead Poet's Society*. They would piggyback off lines in the film like these: "We must constantly look at things in a different way...Just when you think you know something, you have to look at it in a different way even though it may seem silly or wrong, you must try...Dare to strike out and find new ground."[3] The impact of these words lasted much longer than the seconds John Keating (Robin Williams) took to speak them. They were pregnant with power and settled deep into the souls of many viewers, Steve Jobs included, thus shifting our mindset toward change.

Watch the original Apple commercial on YouTube. Notice the way the music playing in the background, the intonations of the narrator, Richard Dreyfus, and the black-and-white images of Einstein, Martin Luther King Jr., Thomas Edison, Gandhi, and others inspire you to believe.

Here's to the crazy ones—
the misfits, the rebels, the troublemakers,
the round pegs in the square holes,

the ones who see things differently.

They are not fond of rules, and they have no respect for
the status quo.

You can quote them, disagree with them, glorify or
vilify them.

About the only thing you can't do is ignore them,

because they change things.

They push the human race forward.

And while some may see them as the crazy ones, we see
genius.

Because the people who are crazy enough to think they
can change the world are the ones who do.

Within 12 months of the campaign's launch, the value of Apple stock had tripled. The "Think different" campaign would come to be known as the marketing that saved Mac, and it is frequently included in conversations about the best marketing campaigns of all time.[4]

Being willing to "think different" can change a lot of what we do and how we produce. And when it comes to your personal comeback, thinking different affects everything. After all, that's what faith is. Joshua had to think different when God told him how to tear down Jericho's walls: March around them, blow trumpets, and shout. Gideon had to think different when he raced out with a skeleton crew and some trumpets, jugs, and torches to face a huge enemy army. Mary had to think different when the angel told her she carried the Son of God in her womb. Martha had to think different when Jesus told mourners to roll the stone away from her dead brother's tomb.

Faith is all about thinking different, about taking God at His unconventional word. In fact, one of the greatest patterns that shows up in Scripture and in life is that God Himself thinks a little different too. He asked Abraham to kill his son, the one who carried the promised blessing, even though God prohibited murder (Genesis 9:5). He delivered food to Elijah using ravens—animals He called unclean. He chose a prostitute, Rahab, in her brothel to hide Israel's spies so they could conquer Jericho. He blessed Solomon with great riches and even greater wisdom even though his parents' relationship began with an illicit affair.

Again and again, God thinks different. That's one reason walking in faith is sometimes so difficult—simply because what God asks us to do is often so different it makes no human sense at all.

Such was the case in the story of the great comeback we are going to explore together in this chapter.

A man named Naaman faced a seemingly irresolvable situation in his life, a problem that just never seemed to get better. Naaman wasn't facing this challenge because of any terrible thing he had done. In fact, we read in 2 Kings 5:1, "Naaman, captain of the army of the king of Aram, was a great man with his master, and highly respected, because by him the Lord had given victory to Aram. The man was also a valiant warrior."

Now, great men are hard to come by. So hearing that Naaman was a great man grabs our attention from the start. We're also told that he was highly honored and that the Lord had used him to deliver a great victory to the army in His name. Naaman had rank, reputation, respect, and religion. No doubt he also had great riches as well. The man was on top of the world.

That is, until we come across the next word in verse 1—"but."

The verse says, "But he was a leper." This small addendum to Naaman's description speaks volumes.

We find a thorough description of leprosy in Leviticus 13. The disease would begin as a spot on the skin that would soon start to spread—not only wide but also deep, rotting the skin from within. Leprosy was an incurable disease. And unlike skin cancer, leprosy was also highly contagious. That's why when leprosy reached a certain stage, people inflicted with it were required to be separated from their family, friends, and coworkers. And so a stigma was attached to leprosy. Lepers were social outcasts.

That explains why that side note about Naaman is so significant. Sure, he had a lot of accolades and only one thing wrong. But that one thing was a whopper. Because eventually, if the disease progressed, Naaman would lose everything he had, and then he'd die.

Naaman's story shows us why we need a comeback. He could do nothing to fix his problem. It was an incurable disease that all the money, power, and influence in the world could not overcome. Maybe that sounds familiar to you. Perhaps you are struggling with something, and you don't know how a solution could possibly come about. If that is you, then you are perfectly situated for God to pull off a comeback in your life.

Big Advice from a Little Girl

An unnamed person in Naaman's story played an important role in his comeback. In Scripture, she is simply called "a little girl." She was captured when an army invaded her land (2 Kings 5:2), and now she served Naaman's wife. The little girl made a simple comment that brought about a huge change. She said to her mistress, "I wish that my master were with the prophet who is in Samaria! Then he would cure him of his leprosy" (verse 3).

This young girl most likely did not have an education. She certainly didn't have any social status or economic standing. She had nothing that would make the world stand up and take notice, but somehow, she came up with a vital piece of advice for one of the most important people in the land.

Why is that significant? Because in Hebrews 13:2 we read, "Do not neglect to show hospitality to strangers, for by this some have entertained angels without knowing it." That's a powerful truth for us to incorporate into our lives. We must always be careful to keep our eyes and ears open and to treat others with respect because you never know when God will send a messenger—an angel—to help you on your way. Or you never know when He will use what we consider to be humble means—or humble people—to bring about big changes in our lives.

God can bring specific answers to your questions or your problems, and He's likely to do it in a way you would not expect. Who would have thought a little servant girl would hold the key to Naaman's cure? When you have an incurable problem, look for God to speak in unusual ways.

The girl in Naaman's case was referring to the prophet Elisha. Naaman heeded her words and asked the king for permission to go see Elisha, and the king of Aram sent Naaman on his way with the equivalent of more than a million dollars. The king valued Naaman so much that he sent the gifts to the king of Israel, hoping he would instruct his prophet to fix the problem for good.

Unfortunately, though, some of the problems we face can't be fixed by money alone. In fact, the king of Israel thought the money was a trick because he knew leprosy could not be cured. He replied to the letter and the money in no uncertain terms: "Am I God, to kill and to make alive, that this man is sending word to me to cure a man of his leprosy? But consider now, and see how he is seeking a quarrel against me" (2 Kings 5:7).

There was no cure for leprosy, regardless of how much money was offered. Naaman and his king had sought the wrong source for their solution, and many of us do the same thing today. Rather than "think different," they used the same kind of thinking they had always used before: "Throw money at the problem, and surely that will fix it."

Elisha heard about what was going on and summoned Naaman. When Naaman reached Elisha's doorway, he discovered that the prophet had an entirely different plan. "Elisha sent a messenger to him, saying, 'Go and wash in the Jordan seven times, and your flesh will be restored to you and you will be clean'" (verse 10).

What comes next shouldn't surprise us. "But Naaman was furious" (verse 11). He was ticked off because this wasn't how he expected to be treated. He was insulted. Elisha hadn't even come to meet him in person—he had sent a messenger out to his very own doorway.

And the message had only made him angrier. This powerful, wealthy, successful man had followed the advice of a little girl, and as a result he was told to go dip in some water seven times, and that would cure his incurable disease. To say those instructions sounded ludicrous would be an understatement. Naaman was a man of great military conquests. He knew plans and strategies— how to make the most of his resources. Dipping in water seven times wasn't going to change a thing, or so he thought. The Bible tells us, "Naaman was furious and went away and said, 'Behold, I thought, "He will surely come out to me and stand and call on the name of the Lord his God, and wave his hand over the place and cure the leper"'" (verse 11).

The answer Naaman received wasn't the answer he had expected. The prophet's approach wasn't the same as this great man's approach. Because of Naaman's history, background, experience, and resources, he didn't buy what the prophet was selling.

Instead, Naaman *thought*. That was his first problem, and it's often our first problem too. IBM encouraged everyone to "THINK," and that's what we naturally do. Yet Naaman's comeback wouldn't occur until he learned how to do more than think. He needed to learn how to let go of his normal beliefs and "think different." Some people refer to this as thinking outside the box. If you long for a comeback, if you want God's solution to your problem, one thing you need to get straight from the start is that you must do things God's way. And God's ways are often outside the box.

Naaman didn't like that idea at all. He was offended that the king of Israel would not accept his money. He was insulted that Elisha sent a messenger instead of meeting him in person. He was upset with the prophet's strategy: "Are not Abanah and Pharpar, the rivers of Damascus, better than all the waters of Israel? Could I not wash in them and be clean?" (verse 12). And he was frustrated that after a long trip with an already worn-out body, he seemed no closer to clean health than before.

Naaman didn't turn around quietly and bid his farewell. No, Naaman "turned and went away in a rage" (verse 12). He stormed off, most likely yelling, stomping, and swearing at the messenger who had come on behalf of the prophet. After all, this was Naaman's life. It wasn't just simple advice he wanted. He wanted an effective solution to a complicated and debilitating problem.

Some Great Thing

Naaman was willing to pay for an expensive treatment for his leprosy. He must have thought that with a significant investment, he could buy the cure. But his servants—who were used to living on a lot less than Naaman and with fewer accolades—recognized Naaman's response for what it was: pride.

Naaman thought he knew better than anyone else what needed to happen. He thought he was somehow above "these people" and that he could buy his comeback. But he couldn't. That's why his servants "came near and spoke to him and said, 'My father, had the prophet told you to do some great thing, would you not have done it? How much more then, when he says to you, "Wash, and be clean"?'" (verse 13). Naaman's servants hit right at the heart of the matter.

The solution seemed too simple.

We know this was the heart of Naaman's issue because the servants contrasted Elisha's simple cure, which Naaman rejected, with "some great thing," which Naaman surely would have done. God will regularly put us in a position where we must choose: Will we protect our dignity and remain unchanged, or will we humble ourselves and get rid of our problem? That was the choice Naaman was facing. He felt that the simple solution offered to him was beneath him. He was too big, too important, too significant to trust in something so simple.

When I counsel people who are struggling, this issue of

personal pride and dignity often comes up. People want to hold on to their personal esteem so much that they are not willing to humble themselves and do the simple thing God is asking them to do. It's beneath them. And so they continue to struggle and delay their comeback.

Thankfully, just as Naaman had listened to the little girl earlier, he listened to his servants now. A life-threatening illness will open the ears of almost anyone. In the very next verse, we witness Naaman going down to the river and dipping himself seven times, just as the prophet had directed him to. Keep in mind that God often uses the number seven in Scripture when bringing something to completion. Seven times Naaman dipped in the water. Seven times he swallowed his pride. Waist-deep in the water, in full sight of his entourage and other onlookers, this man with a flesh-eating disease lowered himself down and stood back up seven times.

I can imagine what he must have been thinking each time he came out of the water. His servants were probably holding their breath, watching for any sign of improvement in his skin. Nothing happened the first time, the second time…or even the sixth time Naaman dipped. That wasn't the instruction. Naaman had to dip seven times before experiencing a comeback.

One of the reasons many people don't experience a comeback in their situation at home or at work, in their health or in their finances, or anywhere else is that they go only partway. They will do half or two-thirds of what they know God wants them to do, and then when they quit, they wonder why they don't see the change they thought they would get. But *partway* isn't the instruction. The instruction from God is always complete obedience. God always demands full faith.

Abraham fully obeyed God's direction to sacrifice Isaac, his son. Of course, God eventually saved Isaac by providing a ram for Abraham to sacrifice instead. But notice that Abraham didn't see the ram until he raised the knife—until his obedience was complete. In the same way, your comeback is waiting for your full obedience to whatever it is the Lord is asking you to do. When your obedience is complete, you—like Naaman—can experience a complete comeback. We read about Naaman, "So he went down and dipped himself seven times in the Jordan, according to the word of the man of God; and his flesh was restored like the flesh of a little child and he was clean" (2 Kings 5:14).

Naaman didn't experience just one miracle when he dipped seven times—he experienced two. First, his body was completely healed of its disease. And then came miracle number two—Naaman's condition was actually reversed. We read that "his flesh was restored like the flesh of a little child." The implications of this double miracle are powerful. God turned back the hands of time. He rolled back the clock and restored to Naaman more than what his disease had taken away.

Friend, when you get your comeback, don't just look to God to turn your situation around. Instead, trust Him also to restore the years the locusts have stolen (Joel 2:25). That's how great God is. God is so incredibly awesome, He can not only fix what is wrong but also give you back what you have lost. That's why you should never give up hope, regardless of how long you've struggled. God can turn back the hands of time.

But before He can do that, He needs you to think different. Before God can give you your complete comeback—your double portion—He needs you to set down your pride, dignity, and rationale. God needs you to seek Him and His Word concerning your situation so He can tell you what to do. And then He wants you to obey completely.

Are you struggling in your marriage? Has God asked you to surrender to your spouse or show unconditional love? Then do it. Fully. Are you facing challenges with your finances? Did God instruct you in His Word to honor Him with the firstfruits of what He gives you, even when things are tight? Then do it. Are you not yet living out your personal destiny? Do you feel as if you are wandering with no real intention on this earth? Then seek God and His kingdom first, and He will not only direct your path straight to your destiny but also give you the desires of your heart.

Your comeback is waiting for you to take action. Your comeback is waiting for you to do what God has instructed—and do it completely—even if it makes no human sense at all. Your comeback is waiting for you to think different...in faith.

Reflection and Application Questions

1. Chapter 1 begins by looking at ways Apple chose to "think different" and to encourage others to do the same. Tony then offers biblical examples of God operating outside the box. In what ways did God "think different" in these three situations?

   a. Read Genesis 22:1-14. What was different about God's request to Abraham?

b. Read Joshua 2:1-7. God incorporated Rahab and her home into His plan for Israel's victory at Jericho. In what ways is this different from how God had previously led His people?

c. Read Luke 7:36-50. How did Jesus's response to the sinful woman differ from what was expected in that culture?

2. Walking by faith often requires that we let go of our preconceived notions and expectations.

a. Can you think of a time when you have had to do this? What was the situation?

b. What old ways of thinking might you be challenged to reconsider today?

3. Read 2 Kings 5:2-3. What is surprising about the way Naaman's comeback began?

a. Naaman listened to the advice of a "little girl." How might his example help you to be aware of God's direction in your life?

b. Do you receive advice easily, or is that a challenge? Why can receiving advice be difficult? Take a few moments right now to pray, asking God to open your heart, mind, eyes, and ears to His guidance.

4. Naaman had to dip in the water seven times to receive his healing. This required a great deal of faith.

a. Is God asking you to participate in your own comeback by doing something that doesn't make sense to you? What might be hindering you from obeying Him in faith?

b. What happened when Naaman acted in faith? What would you like to see happen when you take your own step of faith?

5. Tony finishes chapter 1 with these words:

> One of the reasons many people don't experience a comeback in their situation at home or at work, in their health or in their finances, or anywhere else is that they go only partway. They will do half or two-thirds of what they know God wants them to do, and then when they quit, they wonder why they don't see the change they thought they would get. But *partway* isn't the instruction. The instruction from God is always complete obedience. God always demands full faith.

a. Write down a few areas in your life where you need to experience a comeback.

b. Take a moment to ask God to reveal to you what He is asking you to do in full faith and complete obedience. Write each of those things down.

c. As you continue reading this book, consider coming back to this list and adding to it.

2

EMBRACE THE UNUSUAL

One day an employer sent a memo to his employees about a United Fund drive. He insisted on 100 percent employee participation. One employee, however, let his supervisor know he was not going to participate. He had no desire or interest in taking part. Word got back to the owner of the company that one employee was about to spoil his bid for a perfect record of participation, and so he called the employee to his office for a talk.

"I hear there is a problem," the employer said.

The employee shifted his weight in his chair, feeling a bit uncomfortable about being called into the office. "A problem concerning what?" he asked.

"I hear you don't want to participate in the United Fund drive," the employer said.

Oh! Is that what this is about? the employee thought, relieved that this meeting had nothing to do with his work performance.

"Right," he said, "I know it is for a good charitable cause, but I don't want to take part in the fund-raiser," he answered.

The employer leaned forward in his chair, placed his elbows on his desk, and looked deep into the employee's eyes. "Well," he said, pausing for effect, "then I have a dilemma, don't I? Since you don't want to participate, and I want 100 percent participation, I believe we have only two options. Option one is that you can participate. Option two is that I can relieve you of your employment so I still have 100 percent participation. Which would you like to choose?"

The employee took no time to consider his options. "I'll participate," he said quickly.

"I'm glad to hear that. You certainly didn't take long to change your mind," the employer said.

The employee responded, "Well, no one ever explained it to me quite like that before."

How we see, hear, perceive, or understand things often affects how we act. And sometimes, when something is explained a little differently, we can grasp it a lot better. A different explanation might be all you need to help you align your thoughts with God's and to clear the way for your comeback.

Understanding God's Motivation Behind a Comeback

Everyone loves a comeback. The masses cheer for the underdog in sports just so they can get the emotional high of watching a comeback. We tear up and applaud for those who have overcome seemingly insurmountable health issues. When a lost pet is found and returned home, as was the case of one dog stranded at sea after a tsunami in Japan, millions of people tune in to watch their meaningful reunion on social media for years to come.

Something innate within us longs to see or experience a comeback. When all looked lost, we thrill to discover that it's not over after all. That things can turn around, even on a dime, and point us in the right direction. Who can forget the Doug Flutie Hail Mary pass, or the 1980 USA miracle win in Olympic hockey? What about the Kentucky Wildcats rallying from 31 points down with only 15 minutes left in the game? Or the Boston Red Sox coming back from a 0–3 deficit in the American League Championship Series en route to win the World Series? Better yet, the greatest comeback fax imaginable—sent by Michael Jordan—contained just two words: "I'm back."

Comebacks inspire us because they help us believe that whatever we might be facing—whether it's a financial setback, a health challenge, a relational breakup, or simply discouragement—we too can rise once again to the dawn of a new day. If it turned around for them, it can turn around for us. It helps us believe that where we are today does not have to determine where we will be tomorrow. Comebacks give us hope, and hope is the very thing that makes our hearts beat strong.

But we aren't the only ones who love a good comeback. In fact, God Himself is the master at creating comebacks and turning things around. He is the architect of the great reversal, ushering in the defeat of a nine-foot giant by the scrawny boy with five stones. Feeding 5,000 (and then some) with a couple fish and a few loaves of bread. God orchestrated one of the greatest promotions of all time when He took a man from prison to the penthouse, placing

Joseph in the second-highest position in Egypt. Then, of course, the comeback of comebacks—the Savior who was crucified, got up from the grave, ascended to heaven, and sat down at the right hand of God.

Comebacks are God's specialty. They bring Him glory, and I have a hunch they also bring Him delight.

But in our time together in this chapter, I want to take a look at some particular reasons God might like to bring them about. Understanding the reason behind the reversal can open the doors for greater participation in the comebacks you desire in your own life. Remember the employee who saw his participation in the fund drive differently after his employer explained his two options? In a similar way, your perspective can change when you learn about God's motivation for the miraculous according to what He values. Then you can align your thoughts and actions under His, thus ushering in a greater manifestation of His power in you.

Do What Seems Unnatural

Our story takes place on the Sea of Galilee. It is a well-known Bible story, one you may be familiar with already. But let's look at this story through new eyes, looking for the *why* behind the *what*. It will help us discover the reasons God desires to turn things around in our lives.

The scene starts with Jesus conducting a Bible study at the beach. He had climbed into a boat belonging to a man named Simon Peter, pushed it out a little way from the land, and begun to teach the people (Luke 5:1-3). After He had finished His small group discussion and study, Jesus said to Peter, "Put out into the deep water and let down your nets for a catch" (verse 4).

Our scene began as a sermon from the boat to the multitudes, but it concluded with a specific lesson directed at one man. From a message for the masses to a word for one person.

It's one thing to go to church and hear a generic message for everyone, isn't it? It's a whole different ball game when that sermon has your name written on it. Those are the sermons that stick with you. Those are the principles that last in the deepest recesses of your mind. I'm always delighted when someone messages me on social media or stops me in person to tell me how something I preached had their name written all over it. "It's like you were speaking directly to me," they often say. And while I knew nothing of what that person was going through, the Holy Spirit knew it all and applied just the right word at just the right time to just the right person. He highlighted the message or the Scripture and said, "Look here—this is for you!" When God does that, He is usually on the verge of doing something great in your life or bringing you to a point of a critical decision.

This is exactly what happened to Peter on this day.

Jesus turned to Peter and basically said, "Hey, Pete, push your boat out into the deep. Let's catch some fish. Nothing but net!" I can imagine Peter's look when he heard this suggestion. In the middle of the day, in the deep? Right! That's like asking a toddler to slam-dunk a basketball when the rim is at regulation height. It just wasn't going to happen.

Yes, Jesus was a great teacher, and He seemed to know what He was talking about during His Bible study near the shore, but when it came to fishing? I imagine Peter threw a sly look to his fishing partners, maybe with a wink—*This guy can't be for real! But let's humor Him—He seems cool.*

Peter's response is classic, and it reflects what we often think when God asks us to do the unusual. He said to Jesus, "Master, we worked hard all night and caught nothing" (Luke 5:5). In other words, "With all due respect, sir, we know what we're doing. We've been out here all night long. This isn't going to work."

Simon Peter had his own business. In fact, it was a business partnership between James and John, sons of Zebedee, and Simon (Luke 5:10). We can call it the Zebedee Fishing Corporation. These were professional men who fished for a living, made a profit, and did it again the next day. They knew their trade. In fact, they had probably been fishing since they were young. They could do it in their sleep, or at least when they were supposed to be sleeping—at night.

Jesus, on the other hand, was a carpenter. He made furniture—tables, chairs, anything that had to do with carving and shaving wood. That's what Jesus knew. So when the carpenter told the fishermen how, when, and where to catch their fish, Peter sought to set Him straight (with respect, using the term "Master"). He felt that he needed to explain something to Jesus.

After all, Peter wouldn't dare go into Jesus's woodshop and tell Him how to be a carpenter, so why would a carpenter think He knew anything about fishing? On the Sea of Galilee, one didn't catch fish with nets in the deep, and certainly not in the daytime. Nets were for night fishing, and Peter knew that. Not only that, fishing with nets was successful only nearer to the shore, where the fish gathered in schools. When the boat went way out into the deep, the fish didn't gather high enough for the nets to reach them.

What Jesus asked Peter to do went against Peter's experience and reasoning. Peter had been doing this for years. You don't run a successful business if you're not catching fish. What Jesus said just didn't make sense.

Two Signs of a Comeback

How can you know when something special is on the horizon and God is about to do something great—perhaps start a comeback in your life? There are two signs. First, God allows all your efforts to be unsuccessful.

Peter and his crew had worked all night long and caught nothing. They had done everything they were supposed to do, had been trained to do, and had done in the past—yet they had nothing to show for it at all.

It feels bad when you have exerted yourself and nothing is working out, when you have done everything you can do, and you have nothing at all to show for it. When you have gone job hunting and everyone has turned you down. Or when you've done the numbers but none of them seem to be working out. It is discouraging when you have gone to the doctors, tried the medications and alternative methods, and yet your illness won't go away. Or when that relationship won't turn around, or you can't seem to lose the weight. Whatever you've felt when you have tried to achieve something time and time again only to come up short, that's exactly how Peter must have been feeling when Jesus told him to push his boat away from the shore.

At a time like that, you just don't feel like trying again. And trying something that most people would consider ludicrous? Why bother? After being out all night, no doubt the fishermen were tired. You may be tired of trying too. But if you are in a spot like Peter, and what you have been trying hasn't worked, you might not be in a bad spot after all. You may be in the vicinity of something very special indeed.

The second sign of an impending comeback is this: After God allows your efforts to be unsuccessful, He asks you to do something that doesn't make sense. What Jesus asked Peter to do contradicted his experience, knowledge, history, background, and instincts. The problem with relying on our instincts, though, is that our instincts are flawed. They are distorted.

Scientists have known for a long time that we don't always see all there is to see. The phrase "perceptual blindness" refers to our brain's routine function of blocking out visual stimuli that we either do not expect to see or that we feel to be irrelevant. This allows our brains to focus in the midst of so much that can grab our attention.

One popular study documenting this phenomenon involved several students passing a basketball on a court. Viewers were asked to count the number of passes. In the midst of the experiment, a person dressed in a gorilla costume walked directly into the middle of the court, danced around, and then walked off. More than half the viewers failed to see the dancing gorilla![1] Even more people don't see large, unexpected objects (such as a unicycling clown) while talking on their cell phones.[2]

Not only do we block out things our brains determine we do not need to see, but we also fill in gaps where we are truly not seeing anything at all. Each person's eyes come complete with a blind spot. This part of the eye does not have the ability to see. And yet, despite this inability, our brains fill in the missing gaps—even colors, textures, and movement—so we don't notice this blind spot at all.[3]

Yes, we often see what we want to see or what our brain decides we should see. But we don't always see all there is, simply because we are operating on an instinctual level of hunches, predictions, past patterns, and subjective factors. God is the only One with perfect vision. Only He can see beyond the physical, tangible world of our expectations and into the past, present, future, and spiritual dimensions all at once. So when God doesn't seem to make sense, He's probably making the most sense of all.

Our histories, backgrounds, and experiences are real, so we often cling tight to what we know and have learned. This is not a bad thing. But what we see is also distorted by sin (our own and others'), our inability to see beyond what we choose to focus on, and our inability to see beyond our time and place. That's why Paul, who had been taken to the third heaven and had seen things there he could not even describe with words, wrote, "For we live by faith, not by sight" (2 Corinthians 5:7 NIV).

As Peter stood near the beach with Jesus, he surely felt that his history, background, and knowledge had given him plenty of information, so he could tell Jesus that His instructions wouldn't work. But out of respect, Peter continued, "But I will do as You say and let down the nets" (Luke 5:5). So he pushed out into the deep. Note the next verse: "When they had done this, they enclosed a great quantity of fish, and their nets began to break."

It doesn't say, "When they had discussed this," but rather, "When they had done this." Your comeback doesn't come simply because you mentally assent to God's Word and His revelation in your life. It is often tied to an act of faith on your part that demonstrates your faith in Him. When Peter pushed his boat out into the deep and acted by dropping his nets, he got such a catch that even their sturdy fishermen's nets began to break.

If Paul were there, I think he would have called that catch exceedingly, abundantly above all they could have asked or imagined (Ephesians 3:20). Yet Peter got to witness the comeback only after he did something contrary to his own instincts, something that even seemed ridiculous.

Going from an empty boat to a net-breaking catch of fish is an emotional comeback, a career comeback, a financial comeback, and a spiritual comeback. But Peter had to adjust his will to God's will in order to get there. He had to move before he realized that Jesus knew exactly where those fish were all along.

God's Purposes in Your Comeback

God is motivated to give you a comeback for several reasons, but here are four important ones.

To Show You Who He Is

God wants you to know beyond a shadow of a doubt that He knows what He is doing. To do that, He puts you in a situation where your knowledge is not working, and then He asks you to do something that doesn't seem consistent with what you think you know. He contradicts your natural reasoning. So when you discover He knows what He knows, and you don't know nearly as much as you thought you knew, He has demonstrated to you that He is trustworthy.

You can trust God for more things when you experience Him in a comeback. He wants to show you what He knows so you can trust Him more.

To Show You Who You Are

We can tell from Peter's response that Jesus's miracle blew Peter's mind. He was so overwhelmed by the blessing that he "fell down at Jesus' feet, saying, 'Go away from me Lord, for I am a sinful man!' For amazement had seized him and all his companions because of the catch of fish which they had taken" (Luke 5:8-9).

Peter's reaction reveals another reason God desires to bless us in these comeback situations—so we can realize that in His presence, we are nothing but sinful people. He wants us to understand His righteousness, holiness, and purity, and to see that when they are stacked up against ours, we are nothing.

Most people look at their blessings and the comebacks in life as a confirmation of how good they are. They think, "I must have been really great for God to do this for me!" But that's not what Peter said. Peter said, "I must be really sinful to be in the presence of a Man like this and act the way I did."

What was Peter's sin? He told Jesus He didn't know what He was talking about. He'd been out all night fishing and hadn't caught a thing. Whenever you tell God He doesn't know what He's talking about, that's not just a comment or a simple objection. That's a sin. Yes, Peter pushed his boat out, but his response to the blessing—his acknowledgment of his sin—lets us know that he had been just placating Jesus.

The reason Peter was so amazed was that he didn't expect anything to happen.

When God reveals His goodness in your life, it ought to bring you to a place of humility. It is not to show you how great you are. It is to show you how different you are from Him. Peter questioned

Jesus's word simply because it didn't fit his intuition, instincts, and experience. We all commit this sin, and we do it frequently.

God operates on an entirely different level than we do. His plans are not like ours. His ways are not like ours (Isaiah 55:8). When we act as if He doesn't know what He's talking about, we sin. He is faithful to reveal the depths of our sin, and He even does it in the midst of blessing us! The blessings of a comeback make us aware of how much we doubt the God who knows and can do all.

Jesus knew Peter was afraid after what happened. He knew Peter had been humbled by what he saw, so He told him, "'Do not fear, from now on you will be catching men.' When they had brought their boats to land, they left everything and followed Him" (Luke 5:10-11).

Jesus comforted Peter's fears first and then strengthened him, giving him courage and confidence. Whenever a person faces a setback of any kind (such as Peter fishing through the night without catching anything), confidence is often the first thing to go. When confidence wanes, expectations drop. Jesus wanted not only to change Peter's fishing expedition but also to give him confidence. He told him not to fear—from now on he would be catching men.

To Show You Your Purpose

This brings us to another motivation God may have for ushering in a comeback—to make you a blessing to someone else. By turning Peter's situation around, God positioned him to go and do more for Him by being a fisher of men and bringing them to the truth of the gospel. Catching fish is great, but transforming lives for the kingdom of God is important on a completely different level.

Remember, God desires to bring about a comeback in your life so that you can…

- Get to know how much He really knows
- See who you really are in His presence
- Be a blessing to others

The definition of a blessing is enjoying, experiencing, and passing along the goodness of God in your life. If you do not share with others what you have received from God, you've stolen the blessing for yourself. That's a big problem in the body of Christ today. There's nothing wrong with emphasizing personal blessing, restoration, or comebacks. The problem is that they are far too often addressed with only one person in mind—you! God's blessings are always designed to be shared. Otherwise, God's favor doesn't flow freely through His body because it stops with each person.

To Show You How to Follow Him

When Jesus makes Peter a fisher of men, He transforms his natural vocation, catching fish, into an opportunity for ministry. What's funny, at least to me, is that Peter "left everything and followed Him" (Luke 5:11). I'm not sure that would have been my reaction. I know my flesh—as you know yours—and I'm thinking that if I had nets out there that were breaking due to the weight of the fish, I would have offered Jesus a percentage of the company. I would have asked Jesus, "How much of the Zebedee Fishing Corporation do You want? You don't have to work very hard. All You have to do is tell us where the fish are!"

Instead of Jesus saying, "Follow Me," I would have been saying, "Jesus, follow me—we're going to make You a partner! We can build something here!" But Jesus flipped the script and blessed Peter so much that Peter did the unexpected and followed Him.

Far too often, when God blesses us, we cut down on how much we serve Him, serve others, or volunteer at the church or in the community. We try to figure out how we can protect our assets or add to our blessings rather than leaving all to follow Christ. Yet the reason God flips the script in your life and allows you to have a comeback is so you can submit to His lordship—because you trust Him as you follow Him in the next steps He has for you. It's not so you can start hoarding.

We don't read of Peter discussing his condo on the Galilee. Nor do we hear anything about him opening a 401(k) or 403(b) or talking about the mutual fund accounts he will open with the proceeds from his huge catch. Peter, recognizing his sinfulness in the face of a holy God, left everything to follow Christ.

My question to you is this: When God gives you your comeback, will you follow Him, or will you spend all your time counting fish? If you choose to count your fish, you will forget about the One who knew where they were located in the first place. God blesses us so we can serve Him more, not less. He doesn't desire to bless you so you will have less time to pray. He wants to bless you so you will have more time for Him and know the power of prayer. He wants you to realize that when you hear His Word, you obey it, and your comeback occurs, you need to spend all the more time in His Word. God blesses us with comebacks in our lives so we can follow Him.

A Comeback Shared

Few had ever heard of Karen Klein not long ago. In her mid-sixties, she had led a quiet life working as a school bus driver for 20 years, and later as a school bus monitor. Her husband had died long before, so she was unable to retire when most would have thought it was time. Her son had committed suicide as an adult. There wasn't much about Karen's life that would have made anyone take notice.

That is, until the day someone filmed a ten-minute video of Karen dutifully riding on the bus with a group of seventh- and eighth-grade students, faithfully performing her job while enduring an onslaught of vulgar taunts and bullying. "If you don't have anything nice to say," she can be heard quietly stating a few minutes into the video, "then don't say anything at all."

But a group of boys continued, degrading Karen in the most horrific ways.

Karen didn't know she was being filmed. She clocked out that day like any other. But the video was posted on YouTube, and within hours it went viral. To date, it's had nearly ten million views. Southwest Airlines stepped up and gave Karen and her family members a trip to Disneyland in response to what had happened. The school system spoke up as well, expelling the students for a year. But when a 25-year-old Canadian decided to ask for donations to bless Karen in spite of all she had suffered for so long, no one expected what would happen next.

Max Sidorov launched his online campaign, thinking that maybe $4,000 or $5,000 would come in for Karen. But within a month, he raised more than $700,000, donated by people who had seen the video or heard the story and wanted to make a statement against bullying. Because of these gifts, Karen was able, at 68 years old, to retire from her job as a school bus monitor. But she didn't retire from life's responsibilities. She didn't take her comeback and start touring the world or buying new cars and clothes—she didn't even get new carpet for her 46-year-old house. What Karen did is exactly what all of us should do when we are blessed—she used a significant portion of the money to bless others. Karen started the Karen Klein Anti-Bullying Foundation.

In the years since the incident, the foundation has sought to eradicate bullying through education, music, books, and many other means. Karen has become a spokesperson for those who, like her before, felt they had no voice.[4]

When God breaks the nets of your life and gives you the comeback you've long desired, will you take what He has given you and use it just for yourself? Or will you follow Him by helping others who need a comeback?

Reflection and Application Questions

1. Comebacks seem to be God's specialty. They bring Him glory in ways few other things can. The road to success often passes through many different difficulties and failures. In fact, failure is often an ingredient of future success because in it we discover wisdom and self-discipline, and we sharpen our vision for the future. The story of John Mark gives a great example.

a. Read Acts 12:25; 13:5,13; 15:38. According to these verses, what was the progression of John Mark's service as a missionary?

b. Read Acts 13:4-13. We can't know for certain why John Mark abandoned the ministry when he did, but based on the series of events recorded in this passage, why do you think he may have thrown in the towel?

c. According to Acts 15:39-41, Paul and Barnabas disagreed about whether to give John Mark a second chance (a comeback) in his missionary service. What is the outcome of this disagreement?

2. Paul chose not to give John Mark a second chance after he had deserted the ministry. But Barnabas did. Barnabas is known in Scripture as being an encourager (Acts 4:36). In what way is encouragement important when someone has failed?

a. Describe a time in your own life when you failed but received encouragement to bounce back and move on.

b. Consider the people in your life right now. Could someone you know use encouragement from you to try again after having failed in some fashion? Name two practical things you can do or say to help them toward their comeback.

3. Read Philemon 23-24 and 2 Timothy 4:11.

a. Paul had given up on John Mark earlier in their journeys. But how does Paul consider John Mark as part of the mission during the latter part of his life?

b. In what way does John Mark's comeback encourage you as you face your own challenges and setbacks in life?

4. This chapter focused on the story of Peter fishing on the sea (Luke 5; John 21). Describe the situation and the result of Peter following Jesus's instructions.

5. Tony mentions two signs that often reveal that God is setting

you up for a comeback: (1) God doesn't allow anything you do to work, and (2) God asks you to do something that doesn't make sense.

a. Think of a time in your life when all your efforts seemed to produce no results. Then consider whether God was leading you to do something about it in a way that didn't (or doesn't) make sense. Describe that situation and your response.

b. Read 2 Corinthians 5:6-8. In what way is God asking you to live by faith and not by sight? What practical things can you do to demonstrate your faith in response to His instructions?

3

DON'T STAY DOWN

Watch out for Heather Dorniden," Heather heard the announcer say. *Yeah, watch out for Heather,* she thought as she rounded the corner in the final lap of the race.[1] Three runners loomed far in front of her, too far to catch even with a heroic last kick. Or so most people thought.

But not Heather. Not the announcer. And certainly not her parents or the home-team fans in the stands either. Cheers roared for this unlikely contender in what would become a historic race, viewed millions of times over the years.

It's not that Heather wasn't an excellent runner to begin with. She was. In fact, in high school she had been crowned an All-State performer five times. Running now on a track scholarship for the University of Minnesota, Heather had been a favorite to claim the title for the 600-meter event at the 2008 Big Ten Indoor Championships her junior year in college. She was slated as the likely winner. That is, until she fell down.

Partway through the race, Heather's feet tangled with another runner's, sending her sprawling headfirst onto the track. This wasn't a short trip or a slight fall either. She didn't just bounce back up. No, Heather skidded so far that the track left marks across her stomach. She lay there for what seemed like seconds. No one could win a race after falling like that. Or could they?

To Heather, it didn't matter very much that she had fallen down. It mattered more that she got back up because she knew her teammates were in a bid to clinch the Big Ten Women's Championship.

She got up, she would later recount, because she didn't want to let them down. Fall or no fall, Heather was going to finish. And finish she did. She had gone from the lead to now trailing a good 30 meters by the time she got back on her feet, but Heather did something no one else had ever done before. She caught the runners up ahead. All of them.

About midway down the backstretch, she passed the first of the three runners in front of her. Cheers grew thunderous, urging her to do the impossible. Rounding the back corner on the final stretch, Heather then hit a gear she didn't even know she had, propelling her past another runner. With only one more to catch and a final lunge near the finish, Heather reclaimed the lead, finishing first in her heat. Heather's collegiate track team would go on to clinch the Big Ten Women's Championship after all.

But Heather clinched much more than that. Rather than staying down, she dared to come back, inspiring a world to realize that despite falling, you can still win.

"It's something that is completely unexplainable to me besides through a higher power," she would later go on to say. "I feel like the Lord just filled me up and gave me the opportunity to show what amazing things can happen through Him."[2]

Amazing things, indeed. More than she could have imagined—just like another woman whose tenacity and faith brought her a comeback that should also inspire us all—Hannah.

Hannah never ran track like Heather, but she showed no less resolve in seeking the goal her heart truly longed for. She was married to a man at a time in biblical culture when multiple wives was the norm, and Hannah found herself outpaced on the track that mattered most to women at that time—family. Her husband's other wife had already borne him children, "but Hannah had no children" (1 Samuel 1:2).

We know that her husband loved her dearly, because we read that he "would give a double portion, for he loved Hannah, but the Lord had closed her womb" (verse 5). Yet even with her husband's love, children during this time secured a future and a legacy for their parents. Children were an essential part of life, especially as parents aged. Hannah wanted nothing more than to have a child.

Hannah's rival enjoyed witnessing her defeat over and over. Her rival would not be considered a good sport on today's field of play. She was a bully who taunted Hannah regularly. We read, "Her rival, however, would provoke her bitterly to irritate her, because the Lord had closed her womb. It happened year after year, as often as she went up to the house of the Lord, she would provoke her; so [Hannah] wept and would not eat" (verses 6-7).

Hannah was in a desperate situation. Not only that, her struggle—unlike Heather's—went on for years. There's something about a prolonged crisis that drains the hope out of you. It's like sitting in an emergency room and waiting for your name to be called, only to watch everyone else go in one by one. While you are suffering from pain, confusion, and worry, time seems to slow to a crawl. Yet those around you don't even seem to care. You become tired and scared. If you aren't careful, your feelings will soon dominate your faith, and you won't have the strength to get up when it's time to. You will lie facedown under a pile of unmet dreams and expectations.

Hannah had a pretty big problem in her day. She couldn't get pregnant. If a doctor were to examine her, he would have chalked it up to a physical problem. But as we saw in the earlier passages, it wasn't Hannah's body that had betrayed her. Rather, the Lord had closed her womb. Hannah's issue wasn't physical at all. It was spiritual—like so many of the issues we face today. If God has closed your womb, it doesn't matter which doctor you go to because that doctor would have to be able to overrule God. And no one can.

Similarly, the problems, emptiness, barrenness, or complications we face in our own lives aren't always as tied to the physical realm as they may appear. When you examine the struggles in your life, don't merely judge what you are facing by what you can see. Instead, ask if God has something to do with your inability to produce, bear fruit, overcome, or achieve. Hannah's physical limitation and her emotional irritation had a purpose, which God would reveal at a later time. If God has allowed you to face trials and troubles right now, they have a purpose as well, and they might be related to your comeback.

Faith in the Face of Futility

Year after year Hannah went up to the temple to pray. Her emptiness hadn't stopped her from going to church, listening to sermons, or seeking the spiritual life. She hung in there waiting for her change to come. But one day, it all became too much for Hannah, and she broke down in desperation and wept.

Sometimes it is okay to cry. It is okay to reach that point where you admit you cannot go any further, apart from God's intervening hand. Life is hard. Setbacks, breakups, and barrenness leave us all weary. Hannah had had more than she could handle, and Scripture tells us she "wept bitterly" (1 Samuel 1:10).

"Weeping bitterly" is not just when tears are flowing down your face. It means you have reached the end of your rope. It is the deep pain that knows no comfort. In those times, even a hug or a kind word from someone would do little good. Weeping bitterly usually comes when we have lost all hope for change.

In those desperate times, desperate measures—things we normally wouldn't do—come to our mind. Hannah was ready for desperate measures. She made a decision at that moment. She would give her child back to God if He would give him to her at all. She made an oath. We read, "O LORD of hosts, if You will indeed look on the affliction of Your maidservant and remember me, and not forget Your maidservant, but will give Your maidservant a son, then I will give him to the LORD all the days of his life" (verse 11).

Hannah had been praying to get pregnant for years, but this time her prayer took on a whole new intensity. Her desire for a child was so strong that she was willing to let go of the thing she wanted most if she could but have him for a while. Even her demeanor reflected a woman distressed in grief as she made her vow to the Lord. As Hannah prayed at the temple, the priest standing nearby thought she was drunk. We know this because he said, "How long will you make yourself drunk? Put away your wine from you" (verse 14).

Hannah was a mess. But she didn't care what people saw. Sometimes troubles are so difficult that the things we used to concern ourselves with don't seem to matter anymore. Hannah pled before the Lord, making her vow in such a way that those around her thought she had lost her mind. But hearing the priest's concern and knowing his position before the Lord, she replied in her right mind: "No, my lord, I am a woman oppressed in spirit; I have drunk neither wine nor strong drink, but I have poured out my soul before the LORD. Do not consider your maidservant as a worthless woman, for I have spoken until now out of my great concern and provocation" (verses 15-16). The priest heard more than Hannah's words—he heard her heart. He believed her, blessed her, and told her that God would give her the child she longed for.

Scripture records that when Hannah heard what the priest had to say, she believed him and went on her way no longer sad. She had faith that her prayer—her vow—would be answered.

What happened next is often overlooked in the study of the life of Hannah, yet it reveals much about the ingredients of faith. For starters, we read that Hannah ate. She had been so hurt for so long—by her barrenness and by the taunting of her rival—that apparently she had stopped eating for some time. Yet with the news from the priest that her prayer would be answered, Hannah returned to a state of calm that enabled her appetite to come back. She began to feed her body and regain her strength.

Then in the next verse, we discover that Hannah had sexual relations with her husband. For couples who have tried to conceive for year after year, the act of intimacy can become a reminder of their loss and pain. It can turn from the joyous celebration it was intended to be into a routine filled with emptiness and regret. But Hannah and her husband didn't allow the years of barrenness to change their behavior. Upon word from the priest that she would conceive, Hannah and her husband acted in faith.

We often make the mistake of being inactive when we're facing the trials and challenges of life. When the mountain seems too high to climb or too large to move, we sit back and leave it all for God to do. But too often, while we think we are waiting on God, He is actually waiting on us. He is waiting to see if we will take an action of faith, even in the face of the impossible.

Had Hannah not had relations with her husband, she would never have gotten pregnant. Had Heather Dorniden not gotten up from the track, she would have never won. In fact, as Heather neared her thirties, she still raced despite her age, and even made the USA national team for the IAFF World Indoor Track and Field Championships. Hers was an unlikely bid, but she kept training and eventually made it. She later reflected on this in her blog.

> Relying on the Lord's plan does not imply lack of action, but rather an openness for His infinite power, strength, courage, and grace to work through me. I intend to approach these races with confidence and purpose, clothed in the armor of Christ. I will perform to the best of my ability with trust that this is all part of a plan much bigger than me, and I am not alone.[3]

Heather's win was much bigger than her. Hannah's pregnancy was much bigger than her. Your comeback is much bigger than you. God has a plan to influence others through you, and that's why He will often let you get to the point where it's clear He is the One who brought it about. But that will not happen without action tied to your faith.

Faith never implies lack of action. Faith is a participatory sport. It means acting as if God is telling the truth. Or, as I sometimes define it, faith is acting like something is so, even though it is not so, in order that it might be so, simply because God said so.

Hannah did more than sit around and wait for God to send a stork with her special package. She acted on the truth that God was going to give her a son. And then, when He did, she fulfilled her vow and gave him back to Him.

> The woman remained and nursed her son until she weaned him. Now when she had weaned him, she took him up with her, with a three-year-old bull and one ephah of flour and a jug of wine, and brought him to the house of the LORD in Shiloh, although the child was young. Then they slaughtered the bull, and brought the boy to Eli. She said, "Oh, my lord! As your soul lives, my lord, I am the woman who stood here beside you, praying to the LORD. For this boy I prayed, and the LORD has given me my petition which I asked of Him. So I have also dedicated him to the LORD; as long as he lives he is dedicated to the LORD." And he worshiped the LORD there (1 Samuel 1:23-28).

Remember that sometimes, when God has a unique purpose to fulfill, He will allow a unique delay, a setback, or some other difficulty to happen. God didn't respond to Hannah until she made her vow to give back the very thing she wanted the most. But she wasn't willing to give up her son until she reached the point of desperation.

If the Lord has pushed the pause button on your life, don't give up. If He has delayed His answer, don't stop trusting. It may mean He is driving you to a point of spiritual depth and experience with Him that goes beyond the norm. He wants to blow your mind with something—to reveal to you something that is beyond the natural. But far too often we will not open our eyes or our hearts to these depths until things get desperate.

God had a special plan for Hannah's firstborn child, Samuel. Samuel would go on to be an instrumental prophet in the land of the Israelites, influencing generations to come. Yet had Hannah not reached a point of utter despair, she may have held on to Samuel for her own fulfillment.

God may be asking us to let go of something for His sake that we would never let go of without reaching a point of crisis. Isn't that what He made Abraham do? He asked Abraham to sacrifice Isaac—his only son through Sarah, the son he loved. When Abraham, in faith, gave Isaac to the Lord, God gave Isaac back to Abraham (Genesis 22).

Luke 6:38 is a powerful verse on that topic that we often don't understand completely. It says, "Give, and *it* will be given to you. They will pour into your lap a good measure—pressed down, shaken together, and running over. For by your standard of measure *it* will be measured to you in return" (emphasis added). Notice the word "it" in that verse. That's a very powerful two-letter word. Whatever you are asking God to give to you, give *it* to Him. Hannah wanted a child, so she gave God a child. Abraham wanted his promise of legacy, so he gave God the son, through whom that legacy would occur.

Are you relationally barren? Then give of yourself relationally to someone else in need, perhaps a shut-in or an elderly person at a group home. Are you financially struggling? Then by all means be as generous as you can be to someone else in need. Hand over to God the *it* you need, and *it* will be given to you.

When you step out in faith and give out of your lack to someone else, you are demonstrating that you believe God when, based on your circumstances, believing God is the last thing you want to do. You are operating on faith even though you can't see a solution.

Do you need a comeback? Then help someone else come back. The standard of measure you use to give will be the standard of measure by which you will receive in return, and then some. Hannah didn't just give birth to Samuel. She got more than she asked for. In the next chapter of the book named after her son, we read that Hannah "conceived and gave birth to three sons and two daughters" (1 Samuel 2:21). Hannah got a houseful after all.

Help on the Track

Friend, if you are struggling right now and don't know how much more you can take, take heart. Allow yourself to go low, even to the point of weeping bitterly like Hannah. Because that is the point where you will find the freedom to trust God fully. Release the thing you think you need so desperately into His hands and providence. When you do, God will give you the strength to keep going and to reach the goal set before you.

And if, by chance, you can't get back up on your own as

Heather did after her fall on the track, or you can't keep going in your own power like Hannah year after year, God can still provide.

Perhaps through someone else, as in the stories of Myles and Melanie.

Lance Corporal Myles Kerr was eager to beat his fellow Marines in the Jeff Drench Memorial 5K in Charlevoix, Michigan. But then he spotted a nine-year-old boy struggling at the back of the runners. "How you doing, little guy?" the marine asked.

Brandon, the young runner, had lost track of the group he was running with. Seeing the soldier in his fatigues, Brandon asked him, "Sir, will you please run with me?"

Of course Myles would. After all, he was trained to leave no (young) man behind. Myles slowed to a jog, and he Brandon stayed together throughout the race, eventually crossing the finish line together.[4]

Then there was Melanie. She was running in a 2.4-mile state championship race. Hundreds of runners were competing for the coveted title and a chance at a collegiate scholarship. With only a fraction of a mile remaining on this sunny Minnesota day, one runner went down with a devastating injury to her patellar tendon. The senior racer sat there for a moment as other runners passed her by. But then, knowing this was the end of her high school racing career, she struggled back up to try and finish. Yet her injury proved to be too severe. Weeping in pain, she limped as far as she could and then crumpled to the ground, unable to finish on her own.

That's when Melanie came into the picture. And what a picture it turned out to be. "Hop on my back," Melanie urged the crying stranger. A senior, this was Melanie's last race too, but she wasn't about to finish it while leaving someone else helpless.

The runner climbed onto Melanie's back, even though she was much bigger than Melanie. Melanie slowly carried her along the rest of the course and finished 8 minutes and 30 seconds after the winner of the race. The girls were tied for dead last, but they won something greater than a race. They gained grace, a friendship, and hope.[5]

You may be like Heather or Hannah, crumpled in your own pain and trusting God for a comeback. If that is you, then I want to encourage you to never give up. Despite the tears, scars, and what other people may say, listen to the announcer calling from heaven, "Watch out for [your name here]." You're going to make it.

But if your struggles have become too much and, in your tears, you just can't find a way to go on, then ask God to send you a Myles or a Melanie today. Ask for someone who will run with you if you just need the extra company to stay in stride. Or pray for someone who will lift you up and let you hop a ride on their faith. There's no shame in needing help in your comeback. Like little Brandon, muster the courage to ask.

Once you cross that finish line and God has restored your strength, remember what was done for you. And give it to the next person the Lord brings your way.

Reflection and Application Questions

1. Tony uses Luke 6:38 to remind us that the *it* we are seeking ought to be similar to the *it* we are sowing. This is also sometimes known as the "law of the harvest." The same principle shows up in farming: If you plant apple seeds, you won't get a pear tree. You plant what you want to harvest. That's why Jesus said, "Give, and *it* will be given to you" (emphasis added). Your need for your specific comeback will tell you the kind of seed to plant so it will reproduce after its own kind. Read Galatians 6:7. Summarize this verse as it applies to pursuing the path of your comeback.

2. In inductive Bible study—observing, interpreting, and applying a passage without referring to outside sources—the first step is to ask some very basic questions about the passage you are reading. For instance, what does the text say? Try to paraphrase or summarize the passage to gain its context. This is valuable because the all-too-common practice of lifting a

verse out of its context is a dangerous approach that can make the Bible say almost anything a person wants. Using the Bible study principle of context, consider a verse that Christians love to quote and memorize: Philippians 4:19. The apostle Paul made a great promise in this verse: "My God will supply all your needs according to His riches in glory in Christ Jesus." The phrase "according to" means "in keeping with"—in other words, a supply that is in keeping with the God who owns it all. That's exciting, but the preceding 18 verses of Philippians 4 show that this promise of a bountiful harvest is set in the context of faithful giving to God's work, as the Philippians had supported Paul. Thus, if the Lord were to give you the necessities of life—food, clothing, shelter—"according to" your giving to His work, would you have plenty, or would you be hungry, naked, and homeless?

a. Take this concept a step further. If the Lord were to give you the comeback you seek in accordance to what you have invested into the lives of others, what would you receive?

b. What practical steps can you take to invest more in the lives of others?

3. In light of the truths we have learned from Hannah's willingness to give back to God what she wanted most (her son), and how this interlinks with the principle about the law of the harvest, consider steps of obedience you need to take in your prayers for a comeback. In what ways will God benefit by answering your prayer request? Make a list and be sure to tell Him as you pray.

4. Tony asks, "Do you need a comeback? Then help someone else come back." Spend time in prayer asking the Lord to open your eyes to the needs of those around you. Ask for practical ways you can be of service to others as they get back up and come back from life's challenges.

5. List three lessons you have gleaned from Hannah's approach toward her barrenness. How can you apply them to your own mindset on life's setbacks?

4

KEEP MOVING FORWARD

Fourteen-year-old Jonathan Pitre lives with a rare condition called epidermolysis bullosa. You have probably never even heard of it. I hadn't until I ran across Jonathan's moving story of strength, resilience, and an amazing comeback. Jonathan suffers from a disease of the skin. It's not leprosy, but it seems even worse. This disease makes Jonathan's skin so delicate that he literally has to be wrapped in gauze so his skin doesn't peel right off.

Every movement, every breath, every bite, and every drink comes with excruciating pain. Eating and drinking bring about blisters in his mouth and throat. Taking a bath is a horrific experience. Children who suffer from the disease Jonathan has are often called "butterfly children" because they are so fragile, like the wings of a butterfly. But while the skin may be delicate, the heart is strong, according to Jonathan. "As much as a butterfly is pretty yet gentle, we have the heart of warriors," he said. "We are very much stronger than we appear."[1]

Because of Jonathan's determination and willingness to endure what most of us could not, his life has encouraged hundreds of thousands of people. In fact, his favorite hockey team, the Ottawa Senators, recently recognized Jonathan's bravery and courage by naming him an "honorary scout" for a day. Jonathan got to hold a media press conference, field questions, and give his advice for the team. His strength and ability to come back from such an enormous physical setback, day in and day out, brought the hockey team members to tears.

Few of us can relate to the pain that Jonathan and others like him have to deal with every moment. Yet many of us know what it is like to lose hope. To feel like life itself has no cure. To believe that the best is simply a mirage and the pools of happiness have run dry.

When things appear to be getting consistently worse rather than better, your emotions and will are tested. If something does happen to go well, even then a lurch in your stomach may remind you not to expect anything good to last long. "After all," you tell yourself, "something always seems to go wrong."

Undoubtedly that is how a man named Gehazi must have felt after years of suffering with an incurable disease. When we meet Gehazi in the Bible, though, he has not yet entered this difficult trial. He first shows up at the tail end of the story of Naaman, and he is still healthy, vibrant, and somewhat adventurous.

The Old Testament, and the Bible for that matter, is made up of many intriguing and valuable stories. But these are not dry retellings of stories, but rather spiritual principles couched in stories. Stories are the literary devices that communicate great theological and practical truths for our daily lives.

When you read the Scriptures or read about the stories of Bible characters like the ones retold in this book, try not to gloss over them. These aren't just stories of people in a far-off land at a far-off time. Buried in these narratives are beautiful nuggets of truth that, when applied to your own life, could trigger your own personal comeback.

As a whole, the Bible is a complex saga interwoven with twists and turns, ups and downs, and myriads of surprises. This is what we find in the case of the man we are learning about now: Gehazi. His story is unpredictable—and almost unbelievable. His comeback makes most people's comebacks seem like child's play. Only Lazarus, or Jesus Himself, faced greater odds against reversal.

But I'm getting ahead of myself. Let's start at the end of the story on Naaman in the book of 2 Kings. Naaman had received his healing from leprosy by dipping in the river seven times. He had followed through with the prophet's directions in faith, and his reward was his cure. Not realizing that his healing would be free of charge, Naaman had carried with him a considerable sum of money to help facilitate his healing. Based on our current currency rates, the amount he had brought was roughly the equivalent of more than a million dollars. That's no small change, and definitely not a tip. But Elisha didn't want Naaman's money. He wasn't a prophet to be bought at a price. So he refused it.

When Gehazi, Elisha's servant, saw his master refuse the money, he had another idea. He quickly concocted a plan, which we read about in 2 Kings 5.

> But Gehazi, the servant of Elisha the man of God, thought, "Behold, my master has spared this Naaman the Aramean, by not receiving from his hands what he

brought. As the LORD lives, I will run after him and take something from him." So Gehazi pursued Naaman (2 Kings 5:20-21).

In other words, Gehazi knew his master had saved Naaman's life but did not take his money. "How much is a life worth? It has to be worth something," Gehazi thought. So rather than allow Naaman to get away without paying anything at all, Gehazi sought to collect on the gratitude this healing had produced.

The Bible is so rich in depth and details that we often don't catch them all. I want to be certain to point out a particular detail to you. When we compare what Gehazi said in response to Naaman's healing with what Elisha said, we find a resemblance.

Gehazi: "As the LORD lives, I will run after him and take something from him" (verse 20).

Elisha: "As the LORD lives, before whom I stand, I will take nothing" (verse 16).

Both these men claimed the name of the Lord. But the resemblance stops there because Elisha also said, "before whom I stand." Both used the name of God, but Elisha had a sense of divine accountability while Gehazi just used God's name in vain.

The lesson for us is this: Using God's name may make us sound spiritual, but if we don't align ourselves with His will (being accountable to Him in every area of our lives), we won't see the results we hoped for. The power of God's name is connected to the content of His character.

But Gehazi did even more than misuse God's name. He also concocted a lie to get his way. In verse 22 we read that Gehazi spoke these words to Naaman:

All is well. My master has sent me, saying, "Behold, just now two young men of the sons of the prophets have come to me from the hill country of Ephraim. Please give them a talent of silver and two changes of clothes."

First we saw that Gehazi misused God's name, and now we see that he misused his master's name as well. But Naaman had no way of knowing, so he gave him more than he asked—he gave him the clothes and *two* talents of silver.

No harm, no foul, right? The man had been healed. He had the money. What was the big deal in cashing in? Gehazi made it to his home, stashed his loot, and assumed he had gotten away with a grand heist. That is, until Elisha confronted him.

"Where have you been, Gehazi?" Elisha asked.

"Me? Uh, nowhere…" Gehazi replied. "Just…uh, running errands."

Then Elisha said to him, "Did not my heart go with you, when the man turned from his chariot to meet you? Is it a time to receive money and to receive clothes and olive groves and vineyards and sheep and oxen and male and female servants?" (verse 26). Elisha knew Gehazi. Gehazi has no doubt been his servant for some time. When you spend that much time with someone, you learn to read their responses, predict their actions, and discern their hearts. "Did not my heart go with you?" Elisha asked Gehazi. Meaning, "I knew what you were up to the moment you snuck off after that chariot."

Sometimes we think we can get away with things no one sees, but God sees. That's the most important thing to remember. When we do wrong, it is always before the Lord. His heart always goes with us, and He knows what choices we are making and why. Elisha displays a physical, tangible example of this ongoing spiritual reality of our Lord. There is no sneaking with God. There is no such thing as hiding the spoils (Acts 5:3). God sees all, knows all, and responds to all in His time.

The next question Elisha asked Gehazi was, *"Is it a time* to receive money and to receive clothes and olive groves and vineyards and sheep and oxen and male and female servants?"* (emphasis added). Life is often about timing. We want things before God is ready to give them, or before we are actually ready to receive them. If someone is blessed before they are mature enough to handle it, they are likely to waste that blessing or even let it corrupt their character. Maybe you can think of someone who received a substantial amount of money, power, or fame before they were mature enough to handle it well. Perhaps instead of making them a better servant to the King—our Lord—it made them annoying, bossy, demanding, or selfish. God knows about this tendency better than anyone, and He knew Gehazi was not ready for this blessing.

Elisha knew it too. Yes, Gehazi had only asked for some clothes and coin, but Elisha knew he was heading on a downhill journey, from clothes to houses, vineyards, sheep, oxen, and servants. Gehazi's appetite for power and affluence led him toward a slippery slope to destruction.

A lot of us don't get our comeback when we want it simply because it is not yet the right time. We have not yet matured or developed enough to be able to handle it well. God does have a plan and a purpose. But we mess up His blessing when we insist on our own timing and take shortcuts to create our own comeback.

Gehazi may have gotten some new clothes, but he wasn't about to get to wear them. Elisha said, "'Therefore, the leprosy of Naaman shall cling to you and to your descendants forever.' So he went out from his presence a leper as white as snow" (2 Kings 5:27). The sentence was passed immediately. And now Gehazi wouldn't be the only one to suffer from the painful, humiliating, debilitating scourge of leprosy. His children and grandchildren would as well.

Gehazi made one bad decision, and he was cursed to pay for it for generations to come. I wonder if you ever made any bad decisions when you were young or vulnerable to your own sinful nature. Maybe it was a bad decision about your finances, your sexuality, your relationships, your career…and now you just can't seem to get out of the hole that sinful decision left you in. You feel stuck there, you feel as if you've been labeled, and every day you seem to be paying the consequences for your sin.

If you are over the age of 30, I'm sure you know about the woman in the beret—the 22-year-old White House intern who caught the eye of the most powerful man in our country at the time, the president of the United States. Over the course of her internship, they developed a relationship in which she says she fell in love with her boss. Monica Lewinsky's story would later come out to the press, forever associating her with unkind, vulgar labels connected to her blue dress.

She was 24 years old when the story of her illicit relationship with the president broke in the news. Speaking nearly two decades later to an enraptured audience at a recent TED talk, and still healing from the pain, she said of that moment, "At the age of 22, I fell in love with my boss, and at the age of 24, I learned the devastating consequences. Can I see a show of hands of anyone here who didn't make a mistake or do something they regretted at 22?"

No one raised their hand. Monica continued, underplaying that reality with a graceful humility. "Yep. That's what I thought. So like me, at 22, a few of you may have also taken wrong turns…Not a day goes by that I'm not reminded of my mistake, and I regret that mistake deeply."[2]

Monica's scandal broke at a time when our world was transitioning from newspapers, radio, and television to the onset of the digital revolution.

> It was the first time the traditional news was usurped by the Internet for a major news story, a click that reverberated around the world…I went from being a completely private person to being a publicly humiliated one worldwide. I was patient zero of losing a personal reputation on a global scale almost instantaneously…This rush to judgment, enabled by technology, led to mobs of virtual stone-throwers.[3]

Were Christ to draw in the sand in 1998, I wonder how many 24-year-olds would have been innocent enough to actually throw a stone at all (John 8). But the only writing in this situation came from ferocious, ratings-hungry, politicizing media who sought to dismember a young woman publicly to promote their own agendas.

"I was branded as a tramp, tart, slut, whore, bimbo, and, of course, *that woman*," Monica said slowly, methodically, in a practiced voice, perhaps so she would not break down now that America had finally allowed her to use her voice.

I was seen by many but actually known by few. And I
get it: it was easy to forget that *that woman* was dimen-
sional, had a soul, and was once unbroken. When this
happened to me 17 years ago, there was no name for
it. Now we call it cyberbullying and online harass-
ment...In 1998, I lost my reputation and my dignity.
I lost almost everything, and I almost lost my life.[4]

She was suicidal for years to come—her parents even demanded
that she shower with the door open. Her life spiraled into one of
obscurity and pain, like so many who are now caught in the cross-
fires of cyberbullying—many of whom actually carry out the end-
ing of their days.

Yet Monica's TED Talk has had millions of views (and counting), and she is experiencing a comeback on a scale few of us
would ever have imagined. She is rising from the ashes of shame
to become a respected activist for redemption and against online
bullying.

In her article "What Monica Lewinsky's Comeback Can Teach
Us All," Domonique Bertolucci writes this:

While few of us will ever need to reinvent our lives
after a scandal of the scale Lewinsky endured, the lessons we can learn from her about how to turn your life
around, can be applied to a more "everyday" kind of
crisis: being fired from your job or being embroiled
in a workplace scandal, discovering your partner has
been unfaithful or being caught in an illicit affair, getting drunk and behaving regretfully at a work or social
function, or finding out you have been betrayed or
humiliated by someone you thought you could trust.[5]

This writer isn't the only one speaking about this unlikely comeback. Many other well-known media influencers, such as Barbara Walters, David Letterman, and Bill Maher, have come out to express their "guilt" and to say they regret how they publicly raked her over the coals.[6]

What Monica and the president did was wrong, but none of us are above making mistakes (otherwise known as sinful choices). We are all human. We have all been in need of God's mercy and grace at some point in our lives. If God were to treat us as we treat each other—for our weaknesses and vulnerabilities, lack of wisdom, and sin—none of us would be a candidate for a comeback. But thank God that He is better than us. And in His great mercy, He gives room for growth. Because as Gehazi learned, sinful choices can change your life for a lot longer than you may have ever thought.

When You Can't Come Back

In biblical times, leprosy was more than a disease. Remember, it not only affected you physically, but it also affected you socially. Cyberbullying may not have existed in those days, but lepers were forced to walk around calling out "Unclean! Unclean!" wherever they went (Leviticus 13:45). They were also commanded to live alone, outside of the social structures of that day. A life of constant pain and shame plagued lepers, most of whom sought shelter beyond the city walls, where the garbage was tossed. They lived on the scraps of discarded food.

The damage caused by leprosy can't be reversed. There is no such thing as a comeback from that. Not according to the laws of this world.

If you feel as if you, too, are in an irreversible situation, take heed to Gehazi's story. You may feel that you will always be in debt, that you will always be a failure, or that you cannot bring that child back from abortion or that marriage back from divorce. Forever, you think, you will be an alcoholic or estranged from your loved ones. Forever your reputation will be tarnished, your dignity denied. Your husband beat you, and now your son is beating his wife. You've passed down the irreversible in your family line, and you think it will go on forever.

Those were also Gehazi's feelings as he sat in the trash, skin festering and decaying.

"Irreversible" can lead to the deepest despair. "Irreversible" knows no cure.

Except God.

God knows how to bring about a comeback in even an irreversible situation.

Obeying What Doesn't Make Sense

Fast-forward a few chapters in the story on Gehazi, and we don't find him living in the trash anymore. We don't hear him shouting, "Unclean!" We don't see him weeping in pain. His clothes are not torn. His heart is not empty. He is still called the servant of Elisha, and he stands before the king (2 Kings 8:4). How can that be?

This was a man doomed to a messed-up life, a messed-up family, a messed-up future. Why is he now hobnobbing with the king, talking with him in a civil conversation? How does a leper, who cannot legally live with the people, wind up in this elevated place? The answer is found in a biblical principle that can change your life and, when applied, give you a comeback in a seemingly irreversible situation.

In chapter 8, we read that the king asked Gehazi to tell him about some great things his master Elisha had done. When Gehazi began to recount the story of Elisha bringing a widow's son back to life, and sending her away to sojourn in another land during a seven-year famine, the woman he was speaking about walked into the king's court. At the end of the seventh year, she had returned to her country as the famine in Samaria drew to a close.

If you recall, the number seven in the Bible often stands for completion. Naaman was instructed to dip seven times in the river before he was healed. The Israelites marched for seven days around the wall of Jericho. Joseph had the Egyptians stockpile food supplies for seven years before a famine hit the land. Likewise, Samaria had suffered without food for seven years in one of the worst famines it had ever known. We read that it got so bad, people were buying dove's dung for five shekels of silver (2 Kings 6:25). They bought the dung so they could eat any undigested grain they extracted from it. You may think that is bad, but things got even worse, to the point where people were literally eating their own children (verse 28). What caused the famine? An army of Arameans was encamped against the city and had cut off the food supply.

This is where we discover our clue about how Gehazi went from being a leper and an outcast to conversing with the king. If the people inside the city gates were starving, you can imagine what the lepers had to eat from the trash. Little to nothing at all. That's why we run across some desperate lepers in this narrative in 2 Kings, not long after Gehazi came down with his disease.

> Now there were four leprous men at the entrance of
> the gate; and they said to one another, "Why do we
> sit here until we die? If we say, 'We will enter the city,'
> then the famine is in the city and we will die there; and
> if we sit here, we die also. Now therefore come, and let
> us go over to the camp of the Arameans. If they spare
> us, we will live; and if they kill us, we will but die"
> (2 Kings 7:3-4).

Four lepers stood at the entrance of the gate outside starving Samaria. In today's imagery, this might be similar to finding four homeless people underneath a bridge. But these four lepers came to an interesting conclusion. They realized that if they remained outside the gate, where they belonged due to their disease, they would die. They also realized that if they went to the Arameans' camp, they would die as well, since they come from Samaria. Since they were doomed to die either way, they determined, they might as well die trying.

This gives us valuable insight. When you are in a situation that you feel is holding you hostage, you often have to reach that point of desperation before you stop being willing to settle for your circumstances. It may be bad, but you're alive. It may be hopeless, but you're making it each day. Tragically, many people don't get ahead or discover their comeback because they have decided to settle where they are.

When the four lepers realized they were going to die outside the city gate, they basically said, "Let's take a risk. Let's do something." Neither of their two choices was optimal. Nevertheless, they chose to move rather than succumb to the inevitable.

How much more of a shame is it when a believer in Jesus Christ chooses to settle and succumb to what he or she feels is the inevitable? Always remember that "greater is He who is in you than he who is in the world" (1 John 4:4). You have access to the power of God. Even if all the odds are stacked against you, do something. You can't have worse odds than sure starvation and sure annihilation. Yet the lepers didn't settle. If they were going to die, they would die trying to live. So we read,

> They arose at twilight to go to the camp of the Arameans; when they came to the outskirts of the camp of the Arameans, behold, there was no one there. For the Lord had caused the army of the Arameans to hear a sound of chariots and a sound of horses, even the sound of a great army, so that they said to one another, "Behold, the king of Israel has hired against us the kings of the Hittites and the kings of the Egyptians, to come upon us." Therefore they arose and fled in the twilight, and left their tents and their horses and their donkeys, even the camp just as it was, and fled for their life (2 Kings 7:5-7).

After the lepers chose to move, God helped them. The Bible says the Lord amplified their movement. All they did was get up and start walking, yet when they were walking, the enemy thought they heard the sound of a whole army of horses and chariots. This is similar to the army of angels we read about in chapter 6 when Elisha was trapped by the same army. God put some angels behind the four lepers that caused a disturbance so great it routed the enemy.

But the Lord didn't amplify anything until they moved. Neither does He amplify things in our lives when we are simply settling for our circumstances. As long as you are sitting around feeling sorry for yourself, God will not amplify what you do because you are not doing anything for Him to amplify. You have to take a step of faith if you want to hear Holy Ghost footsteps behind yours. If you want God to overrule your enemy, get moving. You can't sit still and wonder why God is not answering your prayers. Move in faith and give Him something to respond to.

You'll see this occur all throughout the Bible—God often waits for His people to move before He moves. He waits for actions of faith before He responds. Why doesn't God move first? Because if He moves first, you don't need faith. Faith is the movement. Whatever inner prompting urged the four lepers to do the unthinkable, they responded to it in faith. Likewise, when you hear the Holy Spirit calling you toward something in your irreversible situation—and it doesn't make sense—do it. Because when God tells you to move, He's not asking for a vote. He's not asking for majority rule. He's not asking if your friends agree.

When the lepers got to the camp and saw that the enemy had fled, they ate and then took some silver, gold, and clothes.

> When these lepers came to the outskirts of the camp, they entered one tent and ate and drank, and carried from there silver and gold and clothes, and went and hid them; and they returned and entered another tent and carried from there also, and went and hid them (2 Kings 7:8).

These guys had hit the lottery! Seeing that no one was around to stop them, they gathered as much loot as they could and took it where they thought it would never be found. But Gehazi knew better. This is the critical link. He remembered what had happened to him when he stole the silver and the clothes and hid them. Even though Elisha did not see, Elisha still knew. And because he knew, Gehazi was now a leper.

So Gehazi spoke up, "We are not doing right. This day is a day of good news, but we are keeping silent; if we wait until morning light, punishment will overtake us. Now therefore come, let us go and tell the king's household" (2 Kings 7:9). This explains how Gehazi entered the presence of the king.

During this season of consequence and famine, God gave Gehazi a retest. It's the same place—Samaria. It's the same situation—stealing silver and clothes. It's the same strategy—hiding it. But this time, Gehazi passed the test.

God will often test us in the same area where we once failed. He does not care how long it takes for us to pass the test. He will keep retesting until we do. It can be quick, like Naaman dipping seven times. Or it may take up to seven years, as it did for Gehazi. It could take even longer. What God cares about is how much your character has changed. He wants to know if you are a different person than you were when you messed up in the first place. We all commit sin, but are you continuing to commit the same ones? Gehazi didn't want to repeat the past. So he and the other three lepers decided to do the right thing. Contaminated, rejected, and cursed by the Samaritans themselves, the four lepers decided to tell them the good news of the spoils rather than keep it all to themselves.

When you pass your test and God gives you your comeback, always remember that it is not just for you. Your comeback and your blessings are meant to extend through you to others. Shortly before the four lepers made their conquest, the prophet Elisha received a prophecy about a great turnaround for Samaria. A few verses before the account of the lepers in the Bible, we read what Elisha shared with the king: "Listen to the word of the LORD; thus says the LORD, 'Tomorrow about this time a measure of fine flour will be sold for a shekel, and two measures of barley for a shekel, in the gate of Samaria'" (2 Kings 7:1). In other words, within 24 hours the city would go from famine to feasting.

Hard to believe, but true. It was so hard to believe, the royal officer assigned to the king "on whose hand the king was leaning" called it ridiculous. "It can't happen; it won't happen—even God couldn't do something like that," he said in as many words (verse 2). The problem looked too big to be fixed so quickly.

Elisha's response to the officer is a warning to us all. He said, "Behold, you will see it with your own eyes, but you will not eat of it" (verse 2). Translation: "Since you don't think even God can fix this mess, you are going to see God do it, but you'll take no part in the plunder. He's not fixing it for you."

The following night after the lepers came to the gate to give Samaria the good news, the king's servants took two chariots with horses to confirm their story. They found that "all the way was full of clothes and equipment which the Arameans had thrown away in their haste" (verse 15). When the messengers reported this to the king, he sent the rest of the people to plunder the camp. Within hours, the city was full of food, just as Elisha had prophesied. And what happened to the royal officer upon whose hand the king had leaned? He was appointed to stand at the gate, and he saw the bounty, but he was trampled there and died (verses 17, 20).

When Elisha prophesied about the abundance of food,

everyone else rejoiced. But since this royal officer chose not to believe in such an enormous comeback, he got to see the food but died before tasting it. Everything turned around in a moment. It turned around on a dime. And when the royal officer died, it created a job opportunity in the king's house.

Scripture doesn't spell it out, but four verses later, the king is talking to Gehazi in his court, asking him for tales about Elisha. That leaves something for a sanctified imagination to draw together. Once Gehazi passed his test, his comeback came quickly.

In other words, "irreversible" doesn't always mean irreversible. Gehazi experienced disaster because of a flaw in his character that he needed to fix. As long as that flaw was unfixed, his condition was irreversible. But when he grew in character and faith, he was ready for a comeback.

Has God given you a retest in exactly the same situation where you've failed before? Then He may be preparing you for your comeback. Yet far too many of us never experience our comebacks because we don't pass our retests. We can pray about it all day long, but the question is, did we pass the test? We can go to counseling all day long, but the question remains, did we pass the test? We can talk to our friends all day long, but we have to pass the test.

Israel wandered in the wilderness for 40 years because they couldn't pass the test. Every time God tested them again, they grumbled rather than give thanks. So God said, essentially, "Let's go another round." Then another test. And another. Until eventually all they did was wander round and round.

When God tests us like this, He often doesn't give specific instructions. Remember how in school, whenever you would take a test, the classroom would be quiet? Remember how the teacher was completely silent? This was not the time for the teacher to give you any information, because the test was designed to see what you knew based on what the teacher had already taught you.

The same is often true in the tests we experience in our spiritual lives. God didn't give Gehazi specific instructions to share his plunder and not hide it. In the same way, God often tests us without telling us exactly what to do. You may feel like God is distant when you need Him most, but He may be waiting to see what you will do with the faith you have in Him and the truth He has previously given you.

Never allow the embarrassment of your past sin to hold you hostage to a life of wandering and regret. God is after one thing—a change of heart and character in you. He can restore you, redeem you, heal you, and even promote you if you will say, "God, reveal the flaw in my character that has caused me to make these sinful choices, and correct me so I can become who You want me to be."

God is not in a hurry. He will wait if you do not wish to grow. But if you are tired of living under the circumstances of a failed and painful existence—in any area of your life—then give God the right and permission to develop your character. If you are tired of living outside the camp, outside of God's blessings of goodness and power, invite God to show you where you have failed in the past and how you can grow in the present. Not every trial or problem is a result of our sin, but many are. If this is the case in your life, take heart; God can reverse your situation when you are willing to let Him grow you in the area where you need to grow most.

Reflection and Application Questions

1. Chapter 4 takes us on a journey through some incredible setbacks, stories, and situations. How we respond to our challenges often determines our comeback. Read 2 Kings 5:16,20. Compare and contrast the two people's responses toward God in these verses.

   a. Identify a time in your life when you sought personal gain from God in a way you later regretted. If you cannot identify such a time, ask God to open your heart and eyes to reveal one to you. If you still cannot, try to identify a time in someone else's life where this was evident. What was the result?

   b. What is one principle you can apply to your life from Elisha's approach to personal gain as outlined in 2 Kings 5:15-16?

2. Knowing we are not called to serve Christ out of pride or merely for personal advancement, what should be our motivation for serving Him? Read 1 Peter 4:10-11 and Colossians 3:22-24. Write down what those passages pinpoint as the focus, motivation, and power for our service.

a. In 1 Peter 4:10-11, in what way does the writer connect serving others with serving Christ?

b. What is the ultimate goal of our service to others?

3. In what ways can you increase the likelihood of your personal comeback by giving to others? Consider one intentional thing you can do within the next 24 hours to bring glory to God by bringing good to someone else.

4. Tony touches on the concept of timing in this chapter. We read, "A lot of us don't get our comeback when we want it simply because it is not yet the right time. We have not yet matured or developed enough to be able to handle it well." In what ways do you still need to mature or develop so you can best be prepared for the comeback you desire?

5. God often waits on us to move before coming to our aid or bringing about our breakthrough. Tony's example in this chapter was that of the four lepers moving in the night and the Lord amplifying them to sound like an army in the ears of their enemies. Take a moment to ask God what He wants you to do in obedience to Him. What can you do that He can amplify?

   a. Are you willing to move forward in faith where God directs you? Why or why not?

   b. What might be holding you back from stepping out in faith? Spend a moment asking God in prayer to give you the courage to overcome these hesitations.

5

STARE DOWN THE CHALLENGE

hen you're in a crisis, you can relate to how a boxer feels when he is getting battered in the ring. Sometimes a crisis feels like it's pummeling you from every angle. You can't even see where the next punch is coming from, but sure enough, it comes. You might be overwhelmed and outmatched, but for some reason the referee is not stopping the match. You're trapped in the crisis, but the whistle doesn't come. That is how it feels to be overwhelmed by a situation. That is how it feels to be in desperate need of a comeback.

But there are lessons to be learned in a crisis. It can either take you down and keep you out, or it can make you stronger than ever. Every boxer knows that not every knockdown is a knockout. You have to get back up. That is, when you can.

Manny Pacquiao (also known as PacMan) knows what it's like to not be able to get back up. In the sixth round of a 2012 clash between Manny and Juan Manuel Marquez (JMM), JMM dealt a decisive blow that sent Manny not only down but also out. In fact, he was out cold. As Manny lay there lost to the world, his head on the canvas, it looked as if his once-shining star might be dimming. He had reached his thirties, and it seemed the time might have come to call it a day.

Knockouts will do that to people. Knockouts have a way of stilling the heart and crushing the drive, even in the greatest of boxers. They often have the same impact in life.

But Manny's trainer knew Manny wasn't cut from the same cloth as most. Manny had to learn the art of bouncing back early on when, one of six children in a poor area of the Philippines, he had to drop out of school due to a lack of money. At the age of 14, he had to move out of his home altogether because his single mom could not afford to feed him. He was living on the streets until the government began supporting him, and soon after that he joined its amateur boxing program. Following the tragic death of a close boxing friend a few years later, Manny decided to pursue a professional career in boxing in his friend's memory.

Being knocked out in life and knocked out in the ring made no difference to this man of resolve and dedication. Manny's trainer, Freddie Roach, explains.

> He got knocked out twice before that, early in his career, and when I first took him over he wanted to show me those tapes. I said, "Why are you showing me these tapes?" He said, "Well I want you to see my whole career, I want you to know the good and the bad." There's always good and bad in boxing. Anyone can get knocked out. He understands that. That's why it doesn't really bother him. The first time I got

knocked out it changed my whole life. He deals with it a lot better than most people.[1]

A knockout can change your life—for the better—if you view it through the right eyes. You may be down, but you do not have to be out. Or you may be out, as in the case of Manny Pacquiao in the fight in 2012, but you don't have to stay out. Manny eventually came to and went on to battle back and win three consecutive unanimous decisions.[2] At the time of this writing, he still holds the title of being the only eight-division world champion, the WBO Welterweight Champion, and the fourteenth-highest paid athlete in the world in 2013. Not only that, but Emmanuel (Manny) is a highly respected man. He not only turned his career around by coming back from a knockout but also turned his life around by coming back from the throes of drugs, womanizing, and alcohol. Now that Manny is a professed and practicing Christian, the people around him say he has put those old ways behind him and uses his time outside of training for his family, serving others, and serving God.

> I'm happy because I found the right way, salvation, born again. We are required to be born again, all of us. Christ said unless we are born again we cannot enter the kingdom of God. So it's very important to me. Jesus Christ said: "I am the way and the truth and the life. No one comes to the Father except through me." There is no other way. The only way is through Jesus.[3]

In the few years it took for Manny to turn his life around, he has been elected to the House of Representatives in the Philippines twice, and he has become a dedicated husband to his wife and committed father to his five children—Emmanuel Jr., Michael, Mary Divine Grace, Queen Elizabeth, and Israel.

To say that Manny has experienced a comeback is an understatement. God turned around Manny's career from a knockout blow, and He turned around Manny's life—saving him from his own sin and destruction. In those saving moments, Emmanuel says in a reverent whisper, "I heard the voice of God."[4] A crisis has a way of doing that in our lives—it opens our ears so we can hear God more clearly.

For this reason, setbacks that lead us to a comeback can teach us some of the most valuable truths we could ever learn. In these times we experience the reality of God in a new way, where He is no longer theology on a shelf, a theory in space, or a concept we believe in. But in these times, He reenters our lives in such a concrete and tangible fashion that He becomes real to us like never before.

It's one thing to know God abstractly; it's another to know Him for yourself. You might be able to say, "He's my rock, my sword, my shield—He's my wheel in the middle of a wheel," but when you are in the middle of a crisis, you don't need spiritual serendipities or highfalutin theological vernaculars. In a crisis, you need to see the living God up close and personal. You need the rawness of a real relationship.

Jehoshaphat's Knockout

God is always with us, but sometimes we don't sense His presence in our lives because we're so busy with our own decisions, solutions, and plans. That's why it often takes a crisis to get us face-to-face with God. In order to experience the living God, we often need an experience that calls for that living God to show up.

This is exactly what King Jehoshaphat needed. He may not have been knocked out cold with his head flat on a canvas, but he and his country faced a potential deathblow that no man could fix. We read about this troubling battle in 2 Chronicles 20.

> Now it came about after this that the sons of Moab and the sons of Ammon, together with some of the Meunites, came to make war against Jehoshaphat. Then some came and reported to Jehoshaphat, saying, "A great multitude is coming against you from beyond the sea, out of Aram and behold, they are in Hazazon-tamar (that is Engedi)." Jehoshaphat was afraid (verses 1-3).

When the king himself is afraid, there must be something to fear. Jehoshaphat and his countrymen were in a severe crisis, and he felt overwhelmed. Lives, futures, and the entire kingdom were on the line.

Before we continue, I'll give the bout some context. After a long history of a united kingdom of Israel ruled by Saul, David, and Solomon, Israel had split into two kingdoms. Israel was the kingdom of the north with ten tribes, and Judah was the southern kingdom, including the tribes of Judah and Benjamin. Jeroboam was the first king of the new Israel, and Rehoboam was the first king of Judah.

The northern kingdom was run by idolatrous kings for more than 200 years, and it fell to the Assyrians in 722 BC. The southern kingdom of Judah included the city of Jerusalem, and it was run by a mixture of good and bad kings for almost 350 years before falling to the Babylonians in 586 BC.

Jehoshaphat was one of the good kings of Judah; he reigned for 25 years early in the history of the southern kingdom. Yet at this crossroads of crisis, he almost lost it all.

The Anatomy of a Crisis

Here's how you know when you are really in a crisis—you reach a point of powerlessness that is reflected in your words. "O our God," prayed King Jehoshaphat, "will You not judge them? For *we are powerless* before this great multitude who are coming against us; nor do we know what to do, but our eyes are on You" (2 Chronicles 20:12, emphasis added). You are in a crisis when you feel helpless, hopeless, and powerless. You do not have the wherewithal to change things, reverse them, or correct them at all.

Every one of us has gone through a crisis to some degree, and probably more than one. The world often panics and doesn't know what to do when a crisis hits, when they're faced with overwhelming obstacles. But we as believers should be different in our response to a crisis.

It's intimidating to stare down your opposition and see that they are formidable. You're probably not facing down a mean right hook like Manny in the ring or a crisis of military proportions like King Jehoshaphat, but perhaps you feel surrounded on all sides by those who seek to do you harm. You have almost certainly been at the point where you feel like your life is breaking down all around you. We all have. It could be a health crisis, a relational catastrophe, family meltdown, career issues, dreams lost, or even financial disarray. If you don't know what to do, you're in a crisis.

Because of the unknown and feelings of helplessness, a crisis often brings fear. We become afraid when we don't have the ability to fix our problems. It's a reminder that we are fallible, imperfect people. In these situations, we desperately need the intervention of the Lord to pull off a comeback.

In the verses we just read, we saw King Jehoshaphat in a tough situation that he knew was well beyond his ability to manage. That's why he was afraid. Later, we will see him cry out to the only One who can save a king or a kingdom. But before anything could be corrected, the people needed to make some changes and turn back to the Lord.

Though today's times are different and the situations may vary, we need to follow the same formula for divine intervention in our own personal comebacks. God is always faithful and always present in our circumstances. He doesn't require any secret formula or strategy from us, just a simple returning to our dependence on Him alone, as we will see in this remarkable story of the king.

Faced with this deep and complicated crisis, King Jehoshaphat raised his hands in desperation and recalled the promises of the Lord. He called on his people to seek the Lord as well.

> Jehoshaphat was afraid and turned his attention to seek the LORD, and proclaimed a fast throughout all Judah. So Judah gathered together to seek help from the LORD; they even came from all the cities of Judah to seek the LORD. Then Jehoshaphat stood in the assembly of Judah and Jerusalem, in the house of the LORD before the new court, and he said, "O LORD..."
> (2 Chronicles 20:3-6).

Jehoshaphat's prayer, recorded for us in verses 6 through 12, stands as a model for how to respond to a crisis and appeal to God in our own times of troubles. Yet what Jehoshaphat did *before* he prayed is perhaps just as critical and not to be missed.

Jehoshaphat had a storied past. He hadn't always done things according to God's will. In fact, he once compromised with the wicked in order to achieve God's will (2 Chronicles 19:1-3). Yet in His grace, God did not let him be destroyed when he did these things. In God's grace, He was kind to him because God considered him to be a good man (verse 3). Jehoshaphat had gotten rid of the Asheroth (idols) from the land, and he had set his heart on seeking God. Even though he wasn't perfect and he sinned against the Lord, his heart was turned toward God—and that's what God looked at and responded to.

As you face your crisis, know that even in your own imperfection, if you will begin to seek God and set your heart toward Him, it will make a difference. God never excuses imperfections or sin, but He can withhold His wrath against them. He can register the seriousness of your pursuit of Him and not give you the full consequences that you deserve for your sin.

God saw Jehoshaphat make strides in bringing the nation back to Him. In fact, in the course of time, Jehoshaphat even became radical in his reformation efforts. Why is this important? Many times when we are calling on God in prayer during our crisis, as we will see Jehoshaphat do shortly, God does not respond because we have not positioned ourselves to be heard. It is not that God is unable to hear, but that we have not adjusted our lives under Him, and so we have created our own relational separation from Him (Isaiah 59:2).

Too many believers today want God to adjust to them without them adjusting to God. Jehoshaphat did wrong, yes—but he adjusted his ways and his heart to God, so when his crisis hit, the separation between them had reduced, and God heard and responded to his prayer.

The Anatomy of a Prayer

Jehoshaphat began his prayer by reminding God about Himself. That is an interesting approach and is often seen in the Bible. When God established His covenant with David, the king replied, "O Lord GOD, You are God, and Your words are truth, and You have promised this good thing to Your servant" (2 Samuel 7:28). At the dedication of the temple, Solomon prayed, "O LORD, the God of Israel, there is no God like You in heaven above or on earth beneath, keeping covenant and showing lovingkindness to Your servants" (1 Kings 8:23). When Nehemiah heard a distressing report about Jerusalem, he prayed, "O LORD God of heaven, the great and awesome God, who preserves the covenant and lovingkindness for those who love Him and keep His commandments…" (Nehemiah 1:5).

During our own times of crisis today, let's not skip or neglect this critical principle of prayer. Begin with acknowledging who God is, and you will not only call on God according to truths to which He is bound, but also remind yourself of what He is made of—thus increasing your faith as you pray.

Jehoshaphat prayed, "O LORD, the God of our fathers, are You not God in the heavens? And are You not ruler over all the kingdoms of the nations? Power and might are in Your hand so that no one can stand against You" (2 Chronicles 20:6). He began by pointing out who God Himself said He was—ruler over all, God in the heavens, possessing all power and all might. The king reminded the King that no one could stand against Him.

Jehoshaphat realized that his crisis did not have the final word—just as your crisis does not have the final word. It may feel final because you are overwhelmed and afraid, but never let your feelings sit in judgment over your faith. You must always let your faith sit in judgment over your feelings. I'm not saying to deny how you feel. How you feel is how you feel. We read that even the king was afraid. If you are trembling, you are trembling. But the problem is not in how you feel. The problem comes when you allow how you feel to override your faith.

Jehoshaphat began his prayer by saying what he knew to be true about God. Heaven had the final say, not his enemy. Heaven would make the closing comment, not the opposing army. For you too, heaven will call the shots—because it's not over until heaven has said it's over. This is yet another reason that knowing God and knowing theology is so important. When you bring those truths to bear in the middle of discord, faith will trump fear.

Feelings always follow circumstances. They react. That's why, when you're in the midst of a crisis, you need to remind yourself what is true and real about God—that He rules over all. He rules over your finances, your career, your relationships, your children, your health, and your emotions. And as Jehoshaphat knew, He even rules over all kingdoms and all nations.

Jehoshaphat then proceeded in his prayer to remind God and himself of God's previous exploits. He went back to what God had done. The king recalled God's amazing displays of strength in driving out the people groups who were occupying Canaan, such as the Canaanites, Hittites, Amorites, and Jebusites. Those names may not mean much to most modern readers, but these people had opposed Israel as God's people attempted to take the Promised Land (Joshua 3).

Even though Jehoshaphat was under attack and the land was being threatened, he knew that God had secured victory in the past, as He had promised beforehand. He knew that God kept His promises and would not allow the land to fall into enemy hands forever. He knew this because prior to Jehoshaphat's reign, King Solomon had dedicated the temple to the Lord and prayed over this place of worship for God's people. King Jehoshaphat recalled this prayer in his prayer (2 Chronicles 20:8-9). He made this connection because Solomon's dedication dealt specifically with battle situations.

Years earlier, at that temple dedication, Solomon had spoken of the Lord going out from the temple and fighting battles for His people (2 Chronicles 6:34-35). God told Solomon He would maintain the cause of His people. That promise was part of the very foundation of their worship of God at the temple. Jehoshaphat knew of this communication between God and Solomon, and so he spoke to the Lord about it. When they were being invaded by the enemy, God's Word said that God would defend them.

The next principle of effective prayer in a crisis is this: Jehoshaphat not only knew God's Word but also held God to it. We can also do this whenever we face a problem. God has given us hundreds of promises in His Word, yet they so often go unclaimed simply because we either do not know them or we fail to hold God accountable to them in times of need. But Jehoshaphat knew exactly what God had promised to do, so he threw God's promises of strength, protection, and provision right back at Him, even citing specific examples from history.

After heading back into history, Jehoshaphat brought in his present situation. But he didn't get to the present until he had first acknowledged who God was, what He had done, and what He had promised to do. After all that, it was time to tell God his problem.

> Now behold, the sons of Ammon and Moab and Mount Seir, whom You did not let Israel invade when they came out of the land of Egypt (they turned aside from them and did not destroy them), see how they are rewarding us by coming to drive us out from Your possession which You have given us as an inheritance. O our God, will You not judge them? For we are powerless before this great multitude who are coming against us; nor do we know what to do, but our eyes are on You (2 Chronicles 20:10-12).

Jehoshaphat admitted that they were powerless and they didn't know what to do. But rather than focusing his sight on the problem, he shifted his eyes to God. As long as the enemy can keep your eyes on your issue, you will be looking at the wrong thing. Jehoshaphat moved his gaze from the crisis to the King, where his help would come from.

The Battle Is the Lord's

God didn't take long to respond to a life and a prayer like that. Immediately He spoke to everyone in the assembly, and even singled out King Jehoshaphat by name, instructing them not to be afraid or dismayed. "The battle is not yours, but God's," God said through a prophet (2 Chronicles 20:14-15). He gave them a specific word for their situation. Likewise, when you are in a crisis and in need of a comeback, and you approach God in faith based on His Word, history, character, and promises, He will do the same for you.

God's instructions to the citizens of King Jehoshaphat's kingdom wouldn't make sense to the average person. But then, marching around a wall seven times and blowing some trumpets didn't seem like a good battle plan during the battle of Jericho (Joshua 6). God works in ways beyond what we can comprehend, so it is critical to position yourself to hear directly from Him.

> "'Tomorrow go down against them. Behold, they will come up by the ascent of Ziz, and you will find them at the end of the valley in front of the wilderness of Jeruel. You need not fight in this battle; station yourselves, stand and see the salvation of the LORD on your behalf, O Judah and Jerusalem.' Do not fear or be dismayed; tomorrow go out to face them, for the LORD is with you."
>
> Jehoshaphat bowed his head with his face to the ground, and all Judah and the inhabitants of Jerusalem fell down before the LORD, worshiping the LORD. The Levites, from the sons of the Kohathites and of the sons of the Korahites, stood up to praise the LORD God of Israel, with a very loud voice (2 Chronicles 20:16-19).

Essentially, the Lord held up His hand and said, "I've got this."

He told the king and his people that they didn't need to do a thing. He would handle it. All they needed to do was stand there and watch what the Lord would do on their behalf.

I don't know about you, but I'm not sure what I'd think about that battle plan. I mean, it sounds good. God's got it. But in the face of a real army with real weapons and real wrath, would you have wanted to stand there? I don't think most of us would. But that's why many people don't get to witness the impossible comebacks God has to offer. His plan seems too easy or too unusual to trust, and so we hold on to the issue with our own hands. We try to figure a way to solve it ourselves. We don't do what Jehoshaphat and the Levites did—fall to the ground and praise God with a loud voice.

In a football game, when the quarterback hands the ball off to a running back, something amazing happens—all the defenders who were chasing the quarterback start chasing the running back. When the quarterback had the football in his hands, the problem was his. But when he handed the ball off to the runner, his problem suddenly became the other guy's problem.

We often want to hold on to the ball and bear our burdens when God is waiting to take the ball. Faith entails a "hands-off" approach to this game of life. Hand the ball off to God and stop holding on to it until you're tackled. Stand back and watch the salvation of the Lord. God is a bit of a glory hog, and He has every right to be. He likes showing off. But we don't let Him when we refuse to pray and praise. Remember, those are usually the most strategic things we could do in a crisis.

The morning of the battle, the king led well. He took his people out to where the enemy thought they were about to prevail, and he said, "Listen to me, O Judah and inhabitants of Jerusalem, put your trust in the LORD your God and you will be established. Put your trust in His prophets and succeed" (2 Chronicles 20:20). If ever there was a verse to live your entire life by, it would be that one: "Put your trust in the LORD your God and you will be established."

Following this word to the people, the king appointed singers and leaders to go out before the army and "give thanks to the LORD, for His lovingkindness is everlasting" (verse 21). They had a praise service as war came upon them. The enemy raised their bows while God's people raised their voices. They gave thanks even though the battle had not even begun. They gave thanks in faith, knowing they had handed this one off to Almighty God.

What happened next will never appear in a war college textbook. It couldn't have been maneuvered or planned. Only God could have orchestrated such a win.

> When they began singing and praising, the LORD set ambushes against the sons of Ammon, Moab and Mount Seir, who had come against Judah; so they were routed. For the sons of Ammon and Moab rose up against the inhabitants of Mount Seir destroying them completely; and when they had finished with the inhabitants of Seir, they helped to destroy one another. When Judah came to the lookout of the wilderness, they looked toward the multitude, and behold, they were corpses lying on the ground, and no one had escaped (verses 22-24).

Not only was the victory complete, but it took three days for the king and his citizens to collect all the spoils from the enemy who had fallen at their feet.

Are you in the middle of a crisis? Do you need a comeback from what looks like imminent defeat? Then praise the Lord. Magnify His name, and exalt His name forever. Never be too reserved or sophisticated to bless the Lord and give Him the praise He is due.

The Levites praised Him with a loud voice—and they also fell on their faces at times. In spite of your circumstances, praise God without restraint. In the middle of your confusion, bless Him. Despite any financial setbacks or health uncertainties, get down on your knees and honor God with your lips and your heart...and then your lifestyle. Even if your comeback has not arrived, even if you've been knocked down or knocked out, bless His holy name—because He is a great God who will do wonders when you trust Him in faith.

Heaven rules in spite of the situation you face. The problem is not yours. The battle is the Lord's.

Reflection and Application Questions

1. Chapter 5 gives us a glimpse into what appeared to be an impossible situation. King Jehoshaphat and his army faced their opponent with all odds stacked against them. In fact, the king himself prayed these words to God: "We are powerless before this great multitude" (2 Chronicles 20:12). This wasn't a contest that could be won with human ingenuity, skill, or

strength. If the king and his nation were to win, it would have to be because God intervened.

   a. Think of another situation in Scripture where the outcome seemed inevitable but God somehow turned it around. For example, you can read Judges 7, 1 Samuel 17, or Joshua 5:13–6:27. In what way did God intervene to bring about victory?

   b. In what way did the leaders respond to God's direction and intervention?

   c. How can you model their response in your own life?

2. After reading 2 Chronicles 19:1-3, would you classify King Jehoshaphat as an upstanding human being? The passage tells us that he covenanted with the wicked to gain his victory, and yet God ultimately helped him win the battle.

   a. What does this teach us about God's character and how He responds to our personal repentance?

b. What things in your life, past or present, might be displeasing to God? Take a moment to repent to God, and set your heart toward Him from this day forward.

3. Read Isaiah 59:2. What does our intimacy with God have to do with His willingness to hear our calls for help?

4. In 2 Chronicles 20:6, the king begins his prayer to God.

a. What aspects does he focus on first?

b. Why do you think the king chose to remind God of His own character and abilities? How can you integrate this into your own prayer life?

5. Tony reminds us of the importance of holding God hostage to His own words.

> Jehoshaphat not only knew God's Word but also held God to it. We can also do this whenever we face a problem. God has given us hundreds of promises in His Word, yet they so often go unclaimed simply because we either do not know them or we fail to hold God

accountable to them in times of need. But Jehoshaphat knew exactly what God had promised to do, so he threw God's promises of strength, protection, and provision right back at Him, even citing specific examples from history.

a. Take some time to search Scripture for promises related to the setback you are facing. You can start by typing these words into a search engine: "Scripture promises related to [your situation]." After finding verses, write those promises down.

b. Commit to praying those promises daily as you look to God to wage the war of your comeback.

Part 2

INGREDIENTS OF COMEBACKS

6

DEVELOP ENDURANCE

clearly remember watching TV when I was a young boy growing up in Baltimore. From time to time the normal programming would be interrupted by a test of the emergency broadcasting system. Then I would hear a loud, annoying noise for 30 or 60 seconds. I used to hate those tests because they always seemed to come at the worst time, just when you didn't want the show to be interrupted. And since there was never any advance warning that the test was coming, there wasn't any way you could avoid it. The station just broke in and did its test.

The setbacks of life are like that. They often come with no warning, just the announcement: "This is a test." There's often nothing to warn you that the doctor is coming back with a bad report or that your company is downsizing. Life's setbacks just show up at the most inopportune times.

In this chapter I want us to see why God allows setbacks, or trials, in the lives of His children. We see throughout Scripture that trials are an inevitable reality in life, and we read imperatives like this: "Consider it all joy, my brethren, when you encounter various trials" (James 1:2).

Notice the Bible does not say *if* you encounter trials, but *when*. Trials are inescapable. Job said, "Man is born for trouble, as sparks fly upward" (5:7). The only way to avoid trouble is to exit life. Jesus said, "In the world you have tribulation" (John 16:33). You can count on it.

Anyone who tells you, "Come to Christ and leave all your troubles behind" is either intentionally lying to you or has not read the Bible very thoroughly.

But notice something else here. Trials are difficulties we inevitably run into as part of life, not necessarily the problems we create for ourselves. Those kinds of problems are called sin. So if you are going through a tough time right now, don't be surprised. If you have just exited a trial, don't be shocked when the next one arrives. Trials come with living in an imperfect world.

The Greek word used for "trials" here has to do with trouble, tribulation, and difficulties. It's a fairly broad word that can be applied to any number of things, including setbacks. The word literally means "multicolored"—as we might say "blue Monday" or "pink slip." We all know the trials that come in the "color" of physical problems—something wrong with the body that just won't go away.

Trials also come in the "color" of emotional problems. An emotional trial may be something that plagues the mind and heart—a past event you can't forget. Emotional trials also come in the form of discouragement or depression, a darkness of the mind that can color your days gray.

Then there are the financial trials—things like the pink slip that signals the end of a job or red ink that shows you have more bills to pay than resources to pay them. If you have ever been passed over for a promotion or denied a pay raise, you know how financial trials can press in on a life.

Family trials also fit in this multicolored assortment. The death of a loved one or a child who is causing you grief can certainly darken your days. So can marital misunderstandings and parental pain.

This is hardly a catalog of every possible trial or setback we face, but you get the idea. Trials come in a multitude of colors, shapes, and sizes. So, since we can't avoid them, what should we do with them? How can we turn a setback into a comeback?

The Reason for Trials

The Bible doesn't shy away from answering those questions. God is very open about why He puts trials in our path. In fact, He says you can *know* why He puts trials in your life.

Why is it critical to explore those reasons? Because if you are facing a trial and don't know what's going on—if you cannot connect your experience with biblical data—you will be discouraged and overwhelmed by your trial rather than "consider[ing] it all joy" (James 1:2). That joy comes when you realize God is up to something great! And that realization is the key to overcoming trials.

Now, I'm not suggesting you can know everything God knows about why your problem has come. But you can know that your trials come for a purpose, which can make the difference between you staying on top of your trials and your trials staying on top of you.

What you know impacts how you feel. When you know what God wants you to know, you can react differently than you would if you were totally in the dark. So what can we know about God's purposes in life's trials? Scripture gives us three important pieces of knowledge.

To Test Your Testimony

First, know that God places trials in your path to test your faith. When you go through hard times, God is putting your faith on the witness stand. Untested faith is no better than untested love. Anyone can say, "I love you" on a moonlit night with soft music playing in a fine restaurant. But the test of that love comes in the daylight when things don't look so rosy.

Remember, God could have stopped your trial from getting to you. He could have taken it out of your path so you wouldn't encounter it. In fact, in His mercy, God does block an awful lot in our lives. We won't know until heaven how often God protected us from the junk Satan tried to throw in our path.

When God *does* allow a trial to reach us, He does so for a specific purpose. He wants us to know by firsthand experience that testing strengthens our faith.

Trials also test our heart and reveal what is there. Without being tested, we wouldn't know where we are weak and need to fortify ourselves. We wouldn't know what impurities need to be removed from our lives if the fire of trials didn't reveal them. Trials are designed to validate in experience what you declare that you believe. Trials bring you to the point where your faith stands the test, no matter how hot the fire. The apostle Peter wrote that we are "protected by the power of God" when it comes to our eternal salvation (1 Peter 1:5). But in the meantime,

> In this you greatly rejoice, even though now for a little while, if necessary, you have been distressed by various trials, so that the proof of your faith, being more precious than gold which is perishable, even though tested by fire, may be found to result in praise and glory and honor at the revelation of Jesus Christ (verses 6-7).

Now let me remind you about a principle we covered in chapter 4: A good teacher tests students only on information he or she has already taught. A good teacher also wants the students to pass the test. So if you are going through a trial, God has already supplied you with the data necessary to pass the test. And He *wants* you to pass the test of this trial so you can graduate to the next level of spiritual maturity.

You may protest, "But I can't remember everything I've been taught." Then do what you did in school and review what God has been teaching you. Utilize the spiritual disciplines of prayer, Bible study, and fellowship with the body of Christ.

As God's students, we are responsible for passing the tests He gives us. The reason some of us are still at our desks taking the test while the other students have already finished and left the room is that we haven't passed yet. If God has you in a test, He will not let you out of it until you score a passing grade. The test will end when your faith has been tried and proven.

Want a good example of someone passing the test? In the midst of his painful mess, Job declared of God, "Though He slay me, I will hope in Him" (13:15). Job's faith was tested by trial after trial, and he passed the test. Now don't get me wrong. This doesn't mean you have to pretend a trial doesn't hurt. Job was suffering extreme emotional, spiritual, and physical pain. He didn't just apply the power of positive thinking and say, "This doesn't hurt." He admitted his pain, but he still passed the test of faith.

To Increase Your Endurance

Second, God allows trials in order to increase our endurance (James 1:3). This is an important aspect of a mature faith. The word "endurance" here is made up of two Greek words that mean "to remain under." We need to stay put in a trial until its purpose has been accomplished. We are to submit to God's trials the way a patient submits to a surgeon. As you may know, facing surgery can be pretty scary. A nurse comes into your hospital room to prepare you and take your vital signs. Then the orderlies roll you onto another bed to wheel you down to the operating room.

There you are, staring up at the lights, knowing you are about to be knocked out by an anesthetic. Next to you are instruments designed to cut you open. People are whispering around you. Despite all this, you don't jump off the table and run from the operating room. Why? Because you trust the surgeon, and you know you must stay put through this trial if the desired result—your restored health—is to be accomplished.

The Bible says we should not run from trials. Instead, we are to run *through* them to develop our endurance. Let me add here that you don't need to run *to* trials either. Some people actually seem to enjoy suffering. They look for trouble. But you don't need to run toward trials. They'll come running to you.

Recently, I learned a painful, firsthand lesson on the importance of hanging in there during trials. I decided to start getting up early and going to the gym again. So I began a weight-lifting program that first day—curls, bench presses, the whole bit. Twenty-four hours later, I was in a trial! I couldn't walk. I was in so much pain that my wife, Lois, had to button my shirt for me. I can assure you, I wanted to run from that trial. I remember thinking, "I don't have to go through all this pain and work at the gym. I need the extra hour of sleep anyway!" I rejected the thought of going back to the gym.

But because of encouragement from a friend who was working out with me, I went back and lifted more weights. I struggled as I felt the pain. But my friend reminded me, "Keep lifting, because as you work your way through the pain, it will subside and you'll start to develop your muscles. But if you quit it now and ever decide to start again, you'll have to go through the pain all over again."

Weight training relies on resistance to help muscles grow. In the trials of life, God puts weights on you and says, "Keep lifting. Don't quit, even though it will hurt for a while." If you keep on pumping the weight, soon you'll see spiritual muscle appear where flab had been before.

To Develop Your Spiritual Maturity

Why does God test our faith and increase our endurance? So "endurance [can] have its perfect result, so that you may be perfect and complete, lacking in nothing" (James 1:4). God's goal for your trials is your growth into spiritual adulthood. That won't happen without some pain, sweat, and effort. Imagine a young person announcing, "I want to be a physician, but I don't want to spend all those years in medical school!"

We may chuckle at a comment like that. But we do something similar in the spiritual realm when all we can think of is getting out from under our trials as quickly as possible and avoiding future trials. God wants to mature us, not just make us comfortable.

When a butterfly is ready to leave the cocoon, it has to fight its way out. If you open the cocoon to help the butterfly get out, you have doomed that butterfly. It needs the struggle to strengthen its wings so it can fly.

God is too kind and too wise to allow us to remain in spiritual immaturity, whining whenever things don't go our way and demanding what we want when we want it. His goal is that we "become conformed to the image of His Son" (Romans 8:29)—and He will not be satisfied until we get there.

I'm told that when a goldsmith in biblical times tested and refined gold, he would keep purifying it until he could see his face in the gold. In the same way, God Almighty will test you until He sees Jesus Christ in you. When you reflect Christ, God knows you have come through the fire.

The Bible says that we are to hang in there with God, whatever the trial, "until we all attain to the unity of the faith, and of the knowledge of the Son of God, to a mature man, to the measure of the stature which belongs to the fullness of Christ" (Ephesians 4:13). Let me share a good illustration of this verse from the Evans house. My son Jonathan, the youngest of our four children, spent years wanting to be the tallest person in the family. When he got closer in height to Anthony, our oldest son, Jonathan wanted to measure himself against Anthony every day.

Then the day came when Jonathan was taller than Anthony. He was bragging all over the house, so I told him, "Don't brag. You may be taller than Anthony, but I'm still the tallest one in this family."

So every week he'd come and say, "Let's stand back-to-back, Dad." We would stand back-to-back, and I would say, "You're not there yet."

But then the day came when Jonathan hit six feet, one and a half inches. He had outgrown me. He would pass me in the hall at home and say with a smile, "Hey, shorty."

God says, "I want to make you as tall as Christ (in attitudes, actions, character, and conduct), not as tall as your neighbor or your spouse." So don't go around measuring yourself against other people or putting your trials back-to-back against theirs. Other people are not your measure; Jesus Christ is. When you start looking more like Him, you know you are getting there.

So God tests our faith to build up our spiritual endurance so we can become mature in Christ. This means our spiritual resources—not our natural resources—take us through trials. Since that's true, what should be our response to trials? James has three tips for us.

Display Some Joy

How should we respond to trials? James says essentially, "With joy!" (James 1:2). When trials come, instead of getting mad, get glad because you know God is up to something good in your life. But let me repeat the caution I shared earlier: This command does not mean you have to hide the pain of a trial or pretend the pain feels good. The Bible does not say we need to *feel* joyful during the trial, but to consider that trial all joy.

The Greek word for "consider" is an accounting term that means "to evaluate." Accountants evaluate or add up numbers to make the balance sheet come out right. Yet sometimes our trials don't add up from a human standpoint. They don't seem to make sense; the balance sheet seems to be off.

God tells us to put away our human calculator and use His. He wants us to evaluate our trials from the standpoint of joy. That means saying, "God, I know You're at work here. I don't know all You want to do in this trial, but I know You allowed it for my good. So rather than complaining, I'm going to praise You in this situation for what You are going to accomplish in me."

That's using God's accounting system.

In God's accounting system, your outlook determines your outcome. Your attitude determines your actions. This is not about feeling; it's about accounting—evaluating or adding up your trials according to His joy. This kind of joy is a decision of the will.

When you are in the middle of a trial, you don't want your emotions to dictate your actions for the same reason a truck driver on the highway doesn't want his cargo to determine his course. If that cargo starts shifting and sliding, the driver soon has a truck that is out of control, swerving back and forth.

A lot of us are like that truck driver in our lives, especially during setbacks. Our feelings swing us back and forth and take us where they want to go instead of where we need to go. So, even though you may not be particularly happy about your circumstances at the moment, you can decide to be joyful because of what you know.

Remember, happiness is circumstantially driven. It depends

on what happens. But joy is not related to circumstances; it is a decision. Why is it important to be joyful in trials? Because if you aren't, a "root of bitterness" can spring up and spoil your walk with Christ (Hebrews 12:15). When that happens, you lose the provision of grace, which is God's fuel supply to take you through anything He may give you. God gives greater grace in trials, but we nullify that grace when we react with anger or bitterness.

Jesus is our great example here. The Bible says He endured the cross because He foresaw the joy of redeeming mankind (Hebrews 12:2). Jesus wasn't happy about going to the cross. He prayed for His cup of suffering to pass if there was any way it could (Matthew 26:39). But Jesus was still joyful because He was accomplishing His Father's will by redeeming us from sin. He was joyful because He knew that the resurrection was coming and that He was going to be enthroned as King of kings and Lord of lords. Jesus was joyful about Easter Sunday morning, not Good Friday afternoon.

"But that's Jesus," you say. "I'm just a human being." Then let's look to the Bible and find out what one human being thought about a severe trial. I'm thinking of Paul's thorn in the flesh (2 Corinthians 12:7).

Three times Paul asked God to remove his trial, and three times God said no because He had a greater purpose for Paul. He wanted Paul to learn the sufficiency of His grace, to realize that God's power is perfected in human weakness (verse 9).

So Paul counted his trial as joy. He was able to say,

> Most gladly, therefore, I will rather boast about my weaknesses, so that the power of Christ may dwell in me. Therefore, I am well content with weaknesses,

with insults, with distresses, with persecutions, with
difficulties, for Christ's sake; for when I am weak, then
I am strong (2 Corinthians 12:9-10).

Paul wasn't glad for the pain but for the power of God he experienced along with that pain.

Returning to James 1:2, please notice the word "all." "Consider it *all* joy," the Word says—not some joy or partial joy, but all
joy. Think of a mother-to-be in labor. She is experiencing plenty
of pain, but hers is a joyful pain because she is anticipating a joyful result, the birth of her baby. God is using our trials to bring
about the joyful result of Christlike maturity, so we can be joyful
in the meantime.

Ask for Wisdom

In addition to displaying joy in the midst of trials, God urges
us to ask for His help during them. James tells us to ask God, and
He will freely and generously give us His wisdom (James 1:5).
What wisdom do we need to ask God for? Wisdom to know how
to handle the paradox of trials.

Wisdom in Paradox

You may have noticed the paradox in the Bible's advice about
trials. You are in a situation that is stressful and perhaps even physically painful, yet you're supposed to be joyful in the middle of it
all. That seems like a contradiction. How can you "consider it all
joy" when you're hurting? You can't—on your own. So you go to
God and pray, "Lord, make sense of this for me. I know You have
something good in this for me. Help me to see Your plan and Your

hand in this trial. Show me how to respond to get the most out of what You want for me right now." That's seeking God's wisdom.

If you do this, will everything suddenly become perfectly clear? Will you see exactly why God has you in this position? No, the Bible never promises that. But the Bible does promise something better—a generous supply of God's wisdom in answer to your prayer so you will know how to navigate successfully through the trial until you have reached its intended goal. You also have the blessing of knowing that God is bigger than your problems, and He knows how to deliver you.

Wisdom in Community

While you're praying, don't forget the wisdom God has already given you in His Word. Look, for instance, at what Paul says:

> No temptation has overtaken you but such as is common to man; and God is faithful, who will not allow you to be tempted beyond what you are able, but with the temptation will provide the way of escape also, so that you will be able to endure it (1 Corinthians 10:13).

This is a great word of encouragement. Whatever you are facing right now, you are not the only one who has ever faced it. Other people in the body of Christ have been there and have seen God bring them through. You can find those people and stay close to them. In fact, remaining in Christ's body is another indispensable piece of wisdom for overcoming trials and coming back strong.

We can't afford to be "Lone Ranger" Christians. When we hide out and try to handle our trials alone, we can start feeling that

God is picking on us, singling us out for hard trials. But when we remain in fellowship in the body of Christ, we realize God isn't picking on us. His people have a lot of hard-earned wisdom to share with us.

Aren't you glad God limits your load to what you can bear and then gives you other people to help you bear it?

One thing I like about weight lifting is that I don't do it by myself. As I'm straining to do those final repetitions, I start grunting and groaning as the weight becomes more than I can bear. If I were alone at that point, I would probably let the weight drop and crush me. But because my friend is standing over me, he can grab that bar in the nick of time and lighten the load by helping me make my last repetition. Then, when I can't hold the weights any longer, he takes them out of my hands and puts them back on the rack. That's grace. That's what God does for us in trials. When your arms are trembling, when you're grunting and groaning and straining, when you feel like the weight is going to crush you, God steps in and lifts it off you.

Wisdom in Prayer

So pray for God's wisdom. But don't pray halfheartedly, James says.

> Ask in faith without any doubting, for the one who doubts is like the surf of the sea, driven and tossed by the wind. For that man ought not to expect that he will receive anything from the Lord, being a double-minded man, unstable in all his ways (James 1:6-8).

The double-minded person is the split-personality Christian, the one who can't make up his mind. He reminds me of the bumper sticker that says, "I'm not indecisive, am I?"

There are three ways to approach trials. Faith says yes, unbelief says no, and doubt says yes and no at the same time. Double-minded Christians want to do it their way, yet they still want God to do it His way. They want some of God and some of themselves.

But God isn't going to play that game. It's as if He's saying, "If you're going to bring your need to Me, then you have to turn it all over to Me. You can't have it both ways." Many times people who come to me for counseling will say, "Pray that I'll do what God wants me to do." Then after we pray and I show them passages in the Word that specify what God wants in their situation, they go out and do what they want anyway. God has a strong word for people like that: "Don't expect anything from Me."

Now you see why more of us aren't getting more answers to our prayers. Your situation may be God's test in your life to take you to the next level of spiritual maturity. But if you are double-minded about your prayers for deliverance—for instance, if you pray for healing in your marriage but can't make up your mind about whether that marriage is worth the struggle any longer—then you short-circuit God's purpose.

Every time I read about being "driven and tossed by the wind," I remember a cruise Lois and I took to Alaska with some friends from our national ministry. We ran into a horrific storm with waves 35 feet high. The huge cruise ship was tossing back and forth. Food was flying off the table. The stewards were crouching in a corner. People were getting sick all over the place. It was total pandemonium.

In the middle of all this, Lois got a little upset. She was wondering why the captain would take us into this storm since the ship was well equipped with technology to detect and avoid bad weather. So Lois picked up the phone and said, "I want to speak to the captain." She wanted to find out what was going on. The person who answered said the captain wasn't available. But he sent a message to Lois in which he said two things.

His first message was essentially, "You can go back to your cabin and go to sleep because I'm going to be at the helm while you're sleeping, and it's no use for both of us to stay up." And his second message was, "This ship was built with these kinds of storms in mind. It's seaworthy, so you don't have to worry."

We went on to bed that night, and sure enough, the next morning the sea was calm and we were still afloat. God says, "You go to sleep, and I'll stay awake. I planned your life with this storm in mind. You will get through it because I'm at the helm." That kind of comfort and reassurance comes when you seek wisdom from God for your trial. Remember, God is bigger than your trial.

Give God Praise

What else can we do to overcome trials? James's third piece of sound how-to advice is to give God praise.

> The brother of humble circumstances is to glory in his high position; and the rich man is to glory in his humiliation, because like flowering grass he will pass away. For the sun rises with a scorching wind and withers the grass; and its flower falls off and the beauty

of its appearance is destroyed; so too the rich man in
the midst of his pursuits will fade away (James 1:9-11).

In this verse, James names two very common kinds of trials:
the poor person who doesn't have the money he needs to respond
to his trial and the rich person who runs into a problem he can't
buy his way out of. Yet James tells us that we are to praise God in
both of these situations.

Most of us fall into one of these two categories. If you're in
the first category, you can praise God because in Him you have
a resource far beyond what money can buy. I've been there, and
I suspect you have too. The poor person can still say, "Lord, I've
run out of money, but I want to thank You anyway. I thank You
for my health. I thank You for the way You have already taken care
of me. Thank You for food on the table and a roof over my head.
Thank You that I have clothes on my back. Even in my poverty, I
want to praise You."

What about the rich person who has a health problem that
money can't cure or a wayward child whom money can't bring
back home? James says to this person, "Glory in your humility."

In other words, the rich person can say, "Lord, I praise You
that this trial is teaching me I can't just pull out my debit card to
fix everything. I praise You that You are teaching me to lean on
Jesus alone."

So whether you are poor or rich, when the trial comes, give
glory to God. He will lift you to a high position at the right time,
and He will humble you when you need humbling. Give Him
praise either way because He knows exactly what you need. God
lets us come into conflict with earthly things so we might see

eternal things more clearly. And He will keep the trial there until we pass the test.

The Reward for Trials

Here's the good part—the spiritual payoff for handling your trials the way God wants you to handle them. When you hang in there and bear the trial, you get the reward. The Bible teaches, "Blessed is a man who perseveres under trial; for once he has been approved, he will receive the crown of life which the Lord has promised to those who love Him" (James 1:12).

This is sweet. When the trial is finished and the lesson has been learned, then God's approval comes. In school, when you have finished all your classes and passed all your tests, you get to wear a special hat and walk across the stage to receive your prize—your diploma—from the dean of the school.

God's reward for the person who endures trials is the crown of life, the reward of kingly glory and recognition. This reward involves a change in your circumstances. It involves your comeback. You move into the realm of spiritual victory. It took Abraham 25 years to see his promised son come along, but Abraham graduated from his trial. It took Joseph 13 years of slavery and prison in Egypt to finish his trial and graduate to the throne next to Pharaoh. And Moses spent the first 80 years of his life in God's "School for Liberators," but he finally passed all the tests and led Israel out of Egypt.

How long will your setback last? Only God knows. But I do know this: Once you have overcome the trial, you'll see a reward greater than anything you could have dreamed of on your own. But until you pass the test, God is going to keep you in the classroom.

Please don't miss an important point here. God wants you to pass the test—to overcome the trial—not only so He can give you the reward but also so you will learn to love Him more, with Christlike passion and devotion. He puts you in trials to draw you close, to teach you to cling to Him, to grow you into spiritual adulthood, and to bring you along in your journey toward your comeback. Let Him finish His work in you.

Reflection and Application Questions

1. The Christian life is not a sprint; it is a marathon. Possessing the character quality of endurance, and knowing how to use it, is critical to coming back from any setback in life. Read James 1:1-3. The Greek words combined to form "endurance" in James 1:3 mean "to remain under."

   a. Give an example of what it means "to remain under" a difficulty, trial, or setback in a way that honors God.

   b. Give some examples of what it would look like to fail "to remain under" or endure a trial in a way that honors God.

2. God's goal for your growth through setbacks is your spiritual maturity.

a. In what way does practicing endurance develop spiritual maturity?

b. According to Ephesians 4:13, what does spiritual maturity look like?

3. Read Hebrews 12:2.

a. For what reason did Jesus endure the pain, humiliation, and devastation of the cross?

b. What personal lesson can you learn from Jesus's example?

4. In this chapter, Tony writes, "The double-minded person is the split-personality Christian, the one who can't make up his mind. He reminds me of the bumper sticker that says, 'I'm not indecisive, am I?'

There are three ways to approach trials. Faith says yes, unbelief says no, doubt says yes and no at the same time. Double-minded Christians want to do it their way, yet they still want God to do it His way. They want some of God and some of themselves." In what way are you or have you been double-minded?

    a. Describe how double-mindedness can delay your personal comeback.

    b. What steps are you willing to take to move forward in faith and leave double-mindedness behind?

5. Read 2 Timothy 2:8-13. For what reason did Paul cling to a spirit of endurance in his ministry?

    a. How should Paul's motivation for endurance influence your own?

    b. According to this passage, what is the reward for enduring with Christ? In what way does this reward coincide with the ingredients of a comeback?

7

SEEK WISDOM

About a week after our youngest son, Jonathan, got his driver's license, he announced that he wanted to drive the family to downtown Dallas. I got in the passenger's seat, and Lois and our oldest son, Anthony, sat in the backseat.

Lois was sitting behind Jonathan, and not long after Jonathan started driving, we heard agonizing groans coming from that area. If you have ever ridden with a new teenage driver, you know exactly what was going on.

Sometimes those groans turned to specific pleas, such as "Tony, you drive!" One of those groans came when Jonathan turned out of a parking lot and ran right over the curb. This drive—however traumatic for Lois—was a defining moment for Jonathan. He had taken the prescribed driver's training course. He had learned the basics. Now the question was how well he would apply the knowledge he had gained. How would he negotiate the turns in the road, the traffic lights, the expressway ramps, and the traffic conditions he would meet? A driver can't control every situation that arises on the road, but a driver also has a lot of choices to make. He can choose between different routes and avoid wrong turns.

Needless to say, Jonathan was not a perfect driver that night, but he did do better on some points than on others. A lot of people could say this very same thing about their lives. After all, life is a lot like driving. Sadly, many people have not negotiated the roads of life very well. If they could do things over again, they would take a different route in their career or avoid that wrong turn in their marriage.

Since none of us can drive the road of life perfectly, we need divine direction, heavenly help, to negotiate the road ahead. God offers us that help in abundance, just as He offers us His wisdom in abundance. We can't expect to bounce back from a setback without knowing what God's wisdom is and how to tap into it for our lives.

Using our driving analogy, we can say that God's wisdom gives us the ability to steer the car properly, to know when to accelerate and when to apply the brake. Relying on the wisdom God supplies, we learn to use the right gear at the right time and to make the right choices so we go the right way on the right road. The road to your comeback requires wisdom. Wisdom is seeing and interpreting life from God's perspective and then making life's decisions based on that understanding.

We know that wisdom is important because the word "wisdom" itself occurs hundreds of times in the Bible, and more than 100 times in the book of Proverbs alone. God is deeply concerned that we learn to live wisely according to His definition of wisdom.

The Concept of Wisdom

I'm sure you would say you want to be a person God considers wise. So let me ask you this biblical question: "Who among you is wise and understanding? Let him show by his good behavior his deeds in the gentleness of wisdom" (James 3:13).

To appreciate this question and its answer, we need to look at the tongue and the way some people use it both to bless God and to curse others. This should not happen, the Bible says, just as a fountain should not, and in fact cannot, send out bitter and sweet water at the same time (verse 11). Obviously a person whose mouth is pouring out blessing and cursing has taken a wrong turn in life and is badly off course when it comes to living according to God's wisdom. How do we know? Because godly wisdom produces good and gentle behavior that is the exact opposite of the wicked and disruptive effects of a poisonous tongue.

We could go many places in the Scriptures to demonstrate the value of God's wisdom, but I've chosen the book of Proverbs since it was written specifically to tell us what God's wisdom is and how it works. Consider Proverbs 4:7-9:

> The beginning of wisdom is: Acquire wisdom; and with all your acquiring, get understanding. Prize her, and she will exalt you; she will honor you if you embrace her. She will place on your head a garland of grace; she will present you with a crown of beauty.

God says we need to get wisdom before we get anything else. We should value wisdom so much that we make it our primary goal and paramount task in life. Why? Because wisdom is the vehicle that will get you to your comeback. So where do we find wisdom? According to Proverbs...

> Wisdom shouts in the street, she lifts her voice in the square; at the head of the noisy streets she cries out; at the entrance of the gates in the city she utters her sayings...Turn to my reproof, behold, I will pour out my spirit on you; I will make my words known to you (1:20-21,23).

Even though everybody else has an idea and a viewpoint, wisdom shouts to us not to miss what God has for us. Only simpletons, scoffers, and fools would ignore or even despise God's wisdom. In fact, Solomon goes on to warn that it would be disastrous to miss wisdom (verses 24-32). Those who reject God's counsel will fall into calamity one day, and then it will be too late to seek, find, and live by God's wisdom. Those of us who want God's wisdom can rely on His Spirit to help us hear wisdom's voice over the noise of our world.

Please note that we can't conjure up godly wisdom on the spur of the moment. Many wish they could pull the rip cord of God's wisdom when they are falling through the air, but that's not the way it works. We need to value wisdom so much that we make it a way of life, not just a parachute to help us escape disaster.

Scripture makes it clear that wisdom is not a philosophical system that's unrelated to life. At its heart, godly wisdom is the skill of righteous living. In other words, wisdom is effectively applying God's truth to everyday situations, and most definitely to life's setbacks. Those setbacks can increase our emotional involvement, making it easier to lose discernment—and that's where wisdom comes in.

Wisdom is taking the data in your head and getting it down to your feet. With this definition, you can see that wisdom is more than acquiring knowledge. You can go to school and acquire knowledge, but it's possible to have a PhD and yet be at kindergarten level in godly wisdom.

Knowledge and Understanding

Please don't misunderstand: Wisdom does involve acquiring a body of knowledge. Certain information is crucial to gaining wisdom, and that information is found in Scripture. You must know and understand spiritual facts if you are to mature in your faith and become more like Christ. We grow in God's wisdom by learning about His truth—the facts revealed in His Word.

Why is this so important? For example, one reason is that our culture tells us that objective, universal truth doesn't exist. The message of the culture is, "It's only true if it's true for you, and what's true for you may not be true for me." But a body of truth does exist, and it's called the Word of God. Jesus said to God the Father, "Your word is truth" (John 17:17). God's Word is the source of His wisdom.

Some people gain knowledge of God's truth but fail to see the relationship between what they know and what they should do about what they know. These people miss out on acquiring wisdom because they lack understanding. Understanding means taking the body of knowledge you have and doing the right things with it. The Bible refers to this as having the heart to understand what God is saying. Knowledge tells you, "This is true."

Understanding says, "Now that you know what is true, this is what you are supposed to do."

Knowledge gives you the data. Understanding helps you see the relationship between the data and how you should function based on the data. I'll give you a simple illustration.

Imagine a couple who can't pay their bills. In their case, the facts are pretty straightforward. The couple adds up their income and totals their bills and gets a pretty accurate picture of their financial situation. They see exactly how much money they need to cover their bills.

The couple can now outline the financial facts of their setback. The facts—this knowledge—lead the couple to conclude that their problem is simply that they need more money. If they had more money, they could pay off their bills and be debt-free.

But this knowledge alone would not fix the problem because the facts have not led the couple to the proper understanding of their situation. They need to understand *why* they are in debt so they can avoid falling into debt again.

In this case, the real problem is that the couple is not managing their money wisely. They are spending money they don't have by using credit cards and making unwise purchases. So more money would just lead to more debt until the facts of this couple's financial situation led them to the proper understanding of the root problem.

So let's say this couple finally gets the real picture. They begin to understand why they are so deeply in debt. They recognize that they have two underlying problems—they spend too much, and they use credit too much. It dawns on them that unless they do something about their spending habits, having more money won't really help them. They are now on their way to their comeback. They have gained wisdom and understanding.

Applying What We Know and Understand

Most of us know what we ought to do most of the time. We understand what it takes to obey and please God. Positioning ourselves for a comeback means *doing* what we already know we should do. The couple in our illustration doesn't only need more money; they need to commit to wisely handling the money they already have.

Let's talk straight. If you go to God without being willing to act on the knowledge and understanding He has already given you, why should He answer your prayer? Why should He give you more blessings to misuse?

Someone may say, "I need a new mate. My marriage is broken." That may be a fact. Your marriage may be in shambles. But do you understand *why* your marriage is broken, and are you fulfilling your biblical responsibility to help fix what is broken? Until that happens, don't expect much from God. I can't emphasize enough how crucial the application of truth is to the biblical concept of wisdom.

Many of us ask to know God's will by praying, "Lord, lead me." But God will not lead you into His unrevealed will until He knows you're doing something with His revealed will—His Word. He will lead you through what is unclear once you are doing what is very clear.

Some of our prayers for direction go unanswered because God sees we are not doing anything with what we already know. We must make plans according to God's Word, but then we must hand our plans over to God for His adjustment and correction, for our sanctification and growth toward Christlikeness. God will turn your plan into His plan as you build your life on His Word.

When we apply God's wisdom to our lives and live in accordance with what He has spelled out in Scripture, then we are in line for a comeback. Wisdom lets us experience God's will, because wisdom is the application of God's Word to the practical issues of life.

Now that we have grasped something of the concept of wisdom, let's contrast the two kinds of wisdom the Bible describes. It's important that we understand these two kinds of wisdom because they are diametrically opposed to each other.

God's Word teaches that one form of wisdom "is not that which comes down from above, but is earthly, natural, demonic" (James 3:15). In contrast, "the wisdom from above is first pure, then peaceable, gentle, reasonable, full of mercy and good fruits, unwavering, without hypocrisy" (verse 17).

Different Sources

For many reasons, people are often confused about what is and is not from God. But clearly, these two forms of wisdom come from different sources. Look again at the wisdom that is not from God. First, it is "earthly," worldly, from below. Our society, and people in general, are trapped by this way of thinking, and that's not surprising. Unfortunately, a large number of Christians also live by human wisdom rather than by divine wisdom. These believers pay a high price for following the world's wisdom. The Bible says, "There is a way which seems right to a man, but its end is the way of death" (Proverbs 14:12).

We need to determine from which source we will draw our

wisdom. The Bible says, "How blessed is the man who does not walk in the counsel of the wicked, nor stand in the path of sinners, nor sit in the seat of scoffers! But his delight is in the law of the LORD, and in His law he meditates day and night" (Psalm 1:1-2).

You see, "the wisdom of this world is foolishness before God" (1 Corinthians 3:19). On his best day, the unbeliever is still a fool before God if he is disagreeing with his Creator. Human wisdom is basically worthless when it comes to doing what God expects. And the Bible is clear that people apart from God don't know where to find wisdom since only God is all-wise.

As we saw above, earthly wisdom is fleshly, and we need only look around us to find people following fleshly wisdom. Consider the often-asked question, "If it feels so good, how can it be so wrong?" My question to someone who thinks that is, "If it's so right, how come your life is such a mess?"

A fleshly approach to wisdom puts feelings on a higher level than faith. It allows emotion to overrule God's revelation. It says, "What's important is how I feel, not what God says." But godly wisdom says that our feelings must conform to God's revelation. We must adjust our feelings to our faith if we are going to be wise.

I once counseled a woman who was getting ready to marry a non-Christian. Her argument was a familiar one: "If God didn't want me to marry this man, He wouldn't have brought him into my life." That's worldly wisdom. The issue is, what does God's Word say? It clearly says, "Do not be bound together with unbelievers" (2 Corinthians 6:14). This unbelieving man may have captured this woman's thoughts and emotions, but what she needed to say was, "God, by the power of the Holy Spirit within me, I will adjust my feelings to Your Word."

When you can turn to the Holy Spirit and live according to God's revealed will, you are on the road to wisdom. You might also see God do some things in your life you wouldn't otherwise see.

Finally, the Bible also calls this earthly, fleshly wisdom "demonic," straight from hell itself. In other words, there is more behind the world's ideas and philosophies than just human thinking. Satan is the mastermind behind the world's false wisdom.

That's why it's so disturbing that some Christians turn to the horoscope to see what they should do for the day. They know their zodiac sign better than they know the Word. Others turn to palm readers or psychic networks for advice and help. Many people think these activities are harmless, but God's Word teaches otherwise. Consider King Solomon. We read that he had only one flaw. He did what was right before God *except* for the fact that he continued to facilitate the burning of incense and to worship at the high places, where idol worship occurred.

I get the impression that Solomon just dropped by the high places every now and then. That's all. Just like the Christian who only reads the horoscope once a week or calls the psychic network a few times. That's all.

But Solomon's attachment to idolatry—as insignificant as it may have seemed—eventually brought him down. He started marrying pagan women who brought all kinds of idolatry into Israel (1 Kings 11:1-8). The devil doesn't need much of an opening to drive home his hellish wisdom. That's why God told the Israelites that anyone who practices any sort of divination or fortunetelling is "detestable" to Him (Deuteronomy 18:10-12). That's also why God said He would drive the pagan nations out of Canaan: They were worshiping idols.

Appropriately, right on the heels of these words, Moses prophesied, "The LORD your God will raise up for you a prophet like me from among you, from your countrymen, you shall listen to him" (verse 15). This was a prophecy of Jesus's coming. And what did Jesus do when He came? He spoke God's Word, the wisdom from above.

The Word of God—with its account of the life of Jesus, God's Living Word—is the source of the wisdom from above. The Bible commands you to learn the truth, live according to its teachings, and to "set your mind on the things above, not on the things that are on earth" (Colossians 3:2). Only those who are plugged into God's wisdom will know God's power.

But too many of us are like the man who bought a chain saw because the hardware store owner told him he could cut down a lot more trees each day with a lot less effort. This guy had never seen a chain saw before—he had only used an ax—but he bought one. He came back a week later, saying, "Give me my money back. This is a piece of junk. I used this thing all day, and I only cut down one tree. This thing doesn't work."

The clerk was amazed, so he took the saw from the man and pulled the cord. When the chain saw roared to life, the man jumped back and cried, "What's that noise!"

Many of us are like that man. They think they have tried God's wisdom, and they have concluded it doesn't work. They think they have been living God's way, but they're actually still stuck in their old ways. How can that be?

Some believers come out of the world and into the church. But instead of discarding the earthly, natural, and demonic wisdom they learned from and preached in the world, they simply learn a few Bible verses and patch God's Word onto their old ways. But the only way you can know God's power in your life is to use His wisdom His way. And that means totally disregarding worldly, human wisdom, not trying to mix some Christian ideas in with it.

Let me put it another way. Did you realize that a very large percentage of rat bait is good food? The food itself doesn't kill the rats, but rather the very small percentage of poison mixed with it. In the same way, even a little bit of worldly wisdom mixed with God's wisdom spells spiritual death. That's why God wants our wholehearted, unmixed devotion. He wants all of us. Godly and worldly wisdom originate from vastly different, mutually exclusive sources.

Different Methods

Once you see the different sources of earthly and godly wisdom, you won't have any trouble seeing the other points of contrast. Next, these two kinds of wisdom operate in sharply dissimilar methods.

Scripture says that earthly wisdom is characterized by "bitter jealousy" and "selfish ambition" (James 3:14). Jealousy says, "I am upset because you have what I want." Selfish ambition makes me upset because you hold a position I want to hold. That's how human wisdom thinks.

But divine wisdom is gentle, and gentleness is connected to the ability to submit to God. The world doesn't approve of submission to anyone, but Scripture shows us again and again the power that comes with serving and surrendering to God.

Human wisdom says you have to go your own way to get where you want to be. Divine wisdom says, "If I surrender to God, He will take me where He wants me to go. I don't have to worry about it, because God is in control. And I don't have to be jealous of you because God's plans for me are perfect."

Now consider the sharp contrast between the spirit behind earthly wisdom and the Spirit who energizes divine wisdom. We just saw that the spirit behind earthly wisdom stirs up jealousy and selfishness. That's because this wisdom is from the devil, who was jealous of God, and in his ambition tried to topple God from His throne. But divine wisdom comes from the gentle and peaceable Holy Spirit. No wonder His gift of wisdom is characterized by gentleness and peace.

Finally, notice what these two kinds of wisdom produce. The Bible says that human wisdom produces "every evil thing" (James 3:16). Divine wisdom, on the other hand, is the source of "mercy and good fruits" (verse 17). It produces positive things like peace and righteousness. It is pure, undiluted by evil.

Earthly wisdom leads us to "lie against the truth" (verse 14), to use and alter the truth to satisfy ourselves and promote our own agendas. Human wisdom subordinates the truth to personal goals. But godly wisdom lifts up the truth. Clearly, these two kinds of wisdom could not be more different.

Cultivating Godly Wisdom

I hope you're saying by now, "Tell me how to get God's wisdom working in my life!" Let me suggest three ways to cultivate godly wisdom. First, the Proverbs say again and again that wisdom begins with the fear of God. Paul says the problem with mankind is that people have no fear of God (Romans 3:18).

For us, fearing God does not mean running away from Him in terror, but revering and honoring Him. In other words, to fear God means to take Him seriously. We have to stop this "nod to God" way of life, the kind of Christianity that goes to church and gives God a nice spiritual compliment. Instead, let's start saying, "God, if this is what Your Word says, this is what I'm going to do. I am going to stop mixing Your way with my way."

What happens when you're driving down the highway and you see a police car parked by the side of the road? You slow down. Why? The officer might not even be looking at you. That car is just sitting there. But on the side of that car is a symbol of authority that gets your attention whenever you see it. It arrests your focus and may cause you to alter your behavior, so you display a kind of fear of it.

That's the kind of fear we should show toward God. Yet some of us are speeding down the highway of life, and we don't even slow down when God shows up. There's no fear of God in our hearts. He doesn't even arrest our attention. If that's the case, we need to cultivate the fear of God by spending time getting to know Him. As we read His Word, we learn more and more about our God, who is indeed worthy of all glory and honor, all fear and respect.

A second way to cultivate godly wisdom is to abide in God. Again, we can do this by abiding in God's Word. Listen to what God says so you are able to judge things the way God judges them. Also, abide in God's Son. Scripture says that in Christ "are hidden all the treasures of wisdom and knowledge" (Colossians 2:3). The closer you draw to Christ, the more the hidden treasures of His wisdom will be accessible to you. Remember, now that you are a Christian, Jesus Christ lives in you and gives you access to everything He has—including His wisdom.

A third way to cultivate godly wisdom is to act on one of the greatest promises in Scripture. James says, "If any of you lacks wisdom, let him ask of God, who gives to all generously and without reproach, and it will be given to him" (James 1:5).

With that kind of offer on the table, what's holding you back? What is keeping you from seeking God's wisdom for the setback situation you're facing? God is eager to grant you His wisdom. He will give it joyfully, gladly, without putting you down. He will give you more wisdom than you can even think to ask Him for.

If we would ask God for wisdom and apply the wisdom He has already given us in His Word, we wouldn't have to keep coming to Him with the same confession or the same requests for help year after year.

Remember, when you do ask for wisdom, ask in faith without any wavering (verse 6). That's when God will reveal Himself to you. Asking God in faith means that we treat Him like the supreme and sovereign God He is. He is not simply a human being who is going to give you only His opinion or a little short-term assistance.

Asking in faith also means we believe that God is ready and willing to answer our prayer for wisdom. In fact, if you don't ask, God may intensify the setback until you do.

I've taken more than my share of airplane flights. I just buy a ticket and get on the plane. But for me to go from point A to point B, a lot of things have to happen. Hundreds of people have to build the airplane, and somebody has to be trained to fly it safely. Somebody else has to be in the control tower to guide the plane through a safe takeoff and landing.

Many people have to apply a lot of knowledge to get me to my destination, but all I need to know is how to get in touch with a reputable airline. Then I find out where the plane is taking off, and I get on board. Their knowledge makes my flight possible.

With that analogy in mind, know that you don't have to be a rocket scientist to be wise from God's perspective. All you have to do is be in touch with the God who possesses all wisdom and all knowledge. He has all the wisdom you will ever need, but if your life is going to take off—if you are going to get your comeback— you have to go to Him. You have to connect with God and access the wisdom only He provides.

Reflection and Application Questions

1. Read Proverbs 4:7-9.

   a. According to this passage, what is the beginning of wisdom—where do you start?

   b. List some practical steps you can take to acquire wisdom.

2. Read James 3:17. This verse lists eight different characteristics of wisdom. Wisdom is pure, peaceable, gentle, open to reason, full of mercy, full of good fruits, impartial, and sincere. Take some time to consider what the manifestation of each of these qualities would look like in your own life, or where these qualities may be lacking. Make notes beside each quality where you can improve; think of ways you can better express this quality to others through what you think, say, or do.

   a. Pure

   b. Peaceable

   c. Gentle

   d. Open to reason

   e. Full of mercy

   f. Full of good fruits

   g. Impartial

h. Sincere

3. Tony tells us that calling on wisdom in the heat of the moment is not the best way to go. Rather, wisdom needs to be a way of life so it can come through in all your thoughts and choices.

   a. Consider a time in your life when wisdom would have spared you from a setback (either large or small).

   b. Spend a moment listing aspects of wisdom that could have helped in that situation.

4. Knowing what is right or understanding what needs to be said or done is not enough to live a life of wisdom. What critical piece is missing? Taking action based on what is right. Take some time to pray and ask God to show you where you need to include His wisdom in your choices more than you already do. Write down anything He leads you to do.

5. Read the following verses and record what the passage reveals about wisdom. Consider how to apply this wisdom toward the comeback you seek:

   a. Jeremiah 9:24

   b. Proverbs 1:7

   c. Proverbs 15:33

   d. Jeremiah 33:3

8

PRACTICE PATIENCE

D o you know any impatient people? You can probably think of several names without trying too hard. All of us know at least one person who is low on patience. We often describe them as having a short fuse.

But God desires for us to live life at the opposite end of the spectrum. A person who is situated for a comeback must not only learn patience, but also apply it. Nothing can interrupt your path to your comeback like impatience. Impatience is the cause of many disasters, whether they're the result of saying a rash word, trying to force a solution through your own means, or even giving up. To be properly positioned for a comeback in your life, you will have to employ the virtue of patience.

The fascinating New Testament term used for our word "patience" literally means to be "long-fused" or "long-tempered." In the Bible, God calls us again and again to be patient in the face of whatever trial or circumstance He may send our way. There is a reason for this, which we will explore in this chapter.

But first, consider this story. One day a doctor called a patient to tell him, "I have some bad news, and some *really* bad news, for you."

The man gulped and said, "What's the bad news?"

"You only have 24 hours to live," the doctor replied.

"That's awful!" the man cried. "What could be worse than that?"

"Well," the doctor said, pausing, "I should have called you yesterday."

Sometimes life is like that. One day is bad, but the next day is worse. One piece of news is bad, but the next piece of news is worse. One decision is bad, but the next one is worse. We need patience to hang in there when things are going downhill and God's timing is not the timing we want. Otherwise, we may never reach the place of comeback.

Yes, sometimes it seems God is taking an awfully long time to get us where He wants us to go. But if we lose patience, if our fuses are too short and we burn out too quickly, we may miss what God wants us to learn from the situation we're in.

Some people don't like to read about patience because they feel guilty. If that's the case for you, stay with me—I want to help you understand what biblical patience is and how to put it into practice in your life on a daily basis.

How to Practice Patience

Let's begin with a fundamental statement on patience. Scripture says, "Be patient, brethren, until the coming of the Lord. The farmer waits for the precious produce of the soil, being patient about it, until it gets the early and late rains" (James 5:7).

To be patient means to be long-tempered, to hang in there and not let your fuse burn down too quickly. But what does this quality look like while we are waiting for a comeback? How can we practice patience then? The Bible gives us this vivid illustration of farming to help us understand patience, along with some precepts to help us put it into practice.

Our patience is to be like that of a farmer. You can't be a farmer if you're impatient. My son once came home with a school assignment to plant a seed and watch it grow. He planted the seed on Monday, and Tuesday morning he was nearly in tears because nothing had happened yet. He definitely did not have a farmer's patience. A farmer can wait patiently for "the precious produce of the soil" because he has done something important. He has sown the seeds of the crop he hopes to produce.

This illustration helps us understand what the Bible means by being patient until the Lord's coming, as James instructed. Patient waiting does not mean sitting and doing nothing, seeing nothing, thinking nothing. Patience is not meant to result in a passive life. Any farmer who tried to produce a crop by passively waiting would starve to death, as would everyone else who depended on him for food. The farmer's patience comes from understanding his limitations.

A farmer needs to be faithful to till the ground and plant the seed, but he has no control over "the early and late rains." He is totally dependent upon God to supply the rain. And if God doesn't supply the rain, the farmer's work has been a waste of time.

Yet, even if God supplies rain, the farmer will see nothing if he hasn't prepared the ground and planted his crop. So, like the farmer, do all God expects you to do before patience becomes an issue. Once you've sown the seed, you can trust Him to do what is impossible for you to do.

Again, being patient doesn't mean being passive. So if you are waiting for your comeback or are undergoing a trial and you need patience, ask yourself, "Have I done what God has commanded and expected me to do?" If not, perhaps God has not withheld His rain from your crops. Rather, maybe you haven't given Him anything to water.

Keep in mind that God's goal is to perfect you, not just to make you comfortable or help you avoid hard times. Therefore, you need patience as you become positioned for your comeback.

How does the illustration of a farmer relate to the Lord's coming? I believe the Bible is not talking about Christ's second coming in this passage (verses 7-9). Instead, James may be writing about the Lord coming to us here on earth to deliver us through (not necessarily *from*) life's trials. This is not Christ's *ultimate* coming, but an *intermediate* coming—His invasion of your circumstances to deliver you through whatever you are facing and cause a spiritual crop to grow in your life.

A farmer plants to produce growth, not just to fill up time. God sends trials and other challenges your way to produce your growth in grace. Patience will help you wait as He works to produce maximum spiritual growth in you. Then, when the rain comes from heaven, when the Lord comes to invade earth, He will bring forth the crop He wants to produce in you. When that part of the process is complete, you will be ready for your comeback.

Strengthen Your Heart

To have patience, you must also strengthen your heart. Why? Because a weak heart won't hold out in times of personal challenge. God's Word tells us, "You too be patient; strengthen your hearts, for the coming of the Lord is near" (James 5:8).

Strengthening your heart means strengthening yourself spiritually so you can handle the external pressure of the trials. This effort is crucial to your comeback. Many people fall apart during trials because they have not been building themselves up. When a trial or a setback hits, it destroys them. These people with weak hearts know they're not ready for situations like that. Their prayer is, "Lord, please don't try me. I'm not ready yet."

God cannot let a situation like that continue. It would be like a child saying to his mom at the end of the summer, "Mom, please don't send me back to school. I'm not ready yet." That child needs to get ready because school is coming. And setbacks are coming too. So how do you strengthen your heart and prepare? Mary of Bethany shows us. When Jesus came to visit, Mary sat at His feet listening to His words while Martha was busy in the kitchen (Luke 10:38-42). Jesus told Mary she had made the better decision.

Take time to sit at Jesus's feet as Mary did, and you'll become strong in heart. Then you will build up the patience you need to experience your comeback.

Don't Complain

The Bible identifies another key to increasing our patience: "Do not complain, brethren, against one another, so that you yourselves may not be judged; behold, the Judge is standing right at the door" (James 5:9).

This command makes good common sense and good biblical sense. When a situation is tense and everyone is a little edgy, nothing makes things worse like someone complaining about everything in sight. Remember, God is listening to what you say. So be careful about what comes out of your mouth when you're going through a setback. Instead of complaining about the people and circumstances God has placed around you, ask Him to give you patience.

The "Judge is standing right at the door" because He's ready to come and invade your circumstances. When we get upset, we tend to take out our frustration on anyone who is near us. But if He hears you complaining against other believers because of the setback He's given you, you have just become a candidate for judgment. God may come through the door not to aid you or deliver you, but to judge you.

Now you may be saying, "Come on, Tony. Let's be practical. How can I go through a hard setback and not complain?" You can do it when you realize God is doing something great in your life, even in the challenging times. He is undoubtedly using your difficult trial to help you grow. God is at work in your circumstances to bring about something unimaginably good.

That's why the Bible says so much about giving thanks. No matter what you are going through right now, you can find something to give thanks for if you look for it. If you're a parent, you'll recognize that children often become very focused on what they don't have. Then we hear questions like, "When are you going to get me this?" or "Why can't I have that?" Never mind that they get to enjoy three meals a day, they sleep in a safe and warm house, and they have a place to be warm and dry in the winter and cool in the summer. Never mind saying thanks for all that. They want to discuss what they don't have.

That's exactly what we do to God sometimes. But if we spent more time praising Him than complaining, we would get through our trials a lot faster. In the absence of complaining, the essence of patience is doing what we're supposed to do—sowing the seed and strengthening our spiritual life while we wait (without complaining) for God to send the rain.

Some Examples of Patience

In addition to the farmer illustration, the Bible is also filled with real-life models of patience. "As an example, brethren, of suffering and patience, take the prophets who spoke in the name of the Lord. We count those blessed who endured" (James 5:10-11).

Notice how James uses the Old Testament here: He points us back to Scripture and says, "Remember the prophets of God and how they exercised patience!" After all, the history and teachings found in the Old Testament were written for "our instruction" (Romans 15:4). We are to learn from what we read there.

The Old Testament prophets not only waited patiently but also witnessed to or proclaimed God's truth in the meantime. They patiently endured hard times and setbacks as they "spoke in the name of the Lord." God asked Noah to preach righteousness for 120 years without a convert, and Noah patiently obeyed. We count him as blessed because he and his family alone survived the flood.

Elijah also proclaimed the word of the Lord. As a result, Queen Jezebel and King Ahab came after him to take his life. But again and again, God supernaturally intervened and saved Elijah. First,

God sent ravens with food for Elijah, and then the widow of Zarephath fed him.

Later, the prophet Daniel was tested at the hands of an ungodly king named Darius. God didn't keep Daniel from Darius's lions' den. Instead, He joined the prophet there. Daniel not only patiently endured and remained faithful to God, but he was counted as blessed even by the evil king (Daniel 6).

Jeremiah, the "weeping prophet," was lowered into a muddy pit for speaking in the Lord's name. But God sent people to Jeremiah to encourage and strengthen him even in the midst of his tears (Jeremiah 38).

Habakkuk was another prophet who waited for God to bring the justice he was praying for. "How long, O LORD, will I call for help, and You will not hear?" (Habakkuk 1:2). But as he waited on God, his patience helped him to receive God's strength:

> Though the fig tree should not blossom and there be no fruit on the vines, though the yield of the olive should fail and the fields produce no food, though the flock should be cut off from the fold and there be no cattle in the stalls, yet I will exult in the LORD, I will rejoice in the God of my salvation. The Lord GOD is my strength (Habakkuk 3:17-19).

Did you notice that James mentioned suffering along with patience? No one said it would be easy to live with patience. Certainly the prophets never found it easy. But those who endure trials patiently are "blessed." In fact, patience marks the difference between a miserable Christian and a joyful Christian during setbacks. The key factor is not the severity of the situation, but the person's response. Has the individual strengthened his or her heart, or has he or she complained all the way through? If you need encouragement and strength in your trial, look to the prophets' example.

Remember, the prophets were God's witnesses even in their hard circumstances. So if you are going through a hard time, talk about the Lord more, not less. Praise Him more, not less. Share Jesus Christ with others more, not less. Being a witness makes the waiting much better.

The Example of Job

The prophets offer us great examples of patience, but James reminds us that the quintessential illustration of patience is the patriarch Job. "You have heard of the endurance of Job and have seen the outcome of the Lord's dealings, that the Lord is full of compassion and is merciful" (James 5:11).

Most of the book of Job is made up of the accusations of Job's friends and Job's defense of his uprightness. Understandably, Job was distressed and depressed by what God had allowed to happen to him. It's certainly okay to be discouraged when things aren't going well. There's nothing wrong with feeling bad if you have something to feel bad about.

It's even okay to question God when you don't understand what He is doing. We all do it. Plus, God already knows when you're questioning Him in your heart, stumbling around looking for answers to your trial. Your questions are no secret to Him. That's why the Word invites you to ask God for the wisdom you need to persevere and be victorious in times of trial (James 1:5). God knows when you're confused, and He wants you to ask Him for wisdom.

Job's friends thought they had discerned God's perspective on Job's calamities, and they let him know it. This ordeal alone—having to listen to his friends go on and on—is evidence of Job's patience, but it was just the beginning. Consider the statement Job made rather early in his friends' onslaught of words: "Though He slay me, I will hope in Him" (13:15). Job had experienced every calamity possible except death itself. He had been stripped of everything else that made life worth living. Yet Job did not die, because God had His hand on the thermostat of Job's "fiery furnace," and God wouldn't let Satan make the fire any hotter than it already was. In the same way, our sovereign God has His hand on the thermostat of your challenge, and things will only get as hot as He allows.

Still, Job looked at his circumstances and said, "Even if God does the only thing left to me that can be done to me, which is take my life, even then I will go to my grave believing that God is faithful."

My friend, that is enduring patience. No complaining from Job, only praise and trust. But the real significance of Job's story lies not in his calamities or his defense before his friends, but in his deliverance and restoration. His story reveals the real spiritual payoff for patience.

At the culmination of his story, notice that Job freely confessed that God and His ways were far too big for him to figure out. If you want to become exasperated and lose your patience (as well as your mind), just try to figure out everything God is doing and why He is doing it. You'll flip out because God is beyond figuring out. His ways aren't our ways. He is the un-figure-out-able God.

In this, Job gained new insight: "I have heard of You by the hearing of the ear; but now my eye sees You" (42:5).

Take a moment to let that powerful statement sink in. Everything Job thought he knew about God was just hearsay compared to seeing God for himself through the lens of his trial.

What does this statement mean for you? It means you can go to church all year and hear other people talk long and passionately and truthfully about God. You can listen to the pastor's sermons each week, listen to Christian radio every day, and watch every religious program available to you. You can hear all about God and yet never really experience Him for yourself—until you go through a trial.

I'm not saying that someone who hears about God but doesn't experience His presence is not a Christian. Job was a longtime believer—and a strong believer—when his setback hit. But it is possible to know God and yet not really see Him for yourself, not really see how He is working in your life.

That's why God sends you setbacks—so you can see with your own eyes what you hear about God doing in other people's lives. God wants you to see Him for yourself. He doesn't just want you to know about what happened to Job or Noah or Daniel or Habakkuk. He wants you to have your own testimony. To give you this gift, He puts you in a place that demands a comeback. Job received a new view of God, but only in the midst of a great trial.

Notice Job's response when he finally saw God: "Therefore I retract, and I repent in dust and ashes" (42:6). As he saw God more fully, Job also received a new view of himself. Remember, Job was the most spiritual man living at that time. If anyone was already right with God, it was Job. Even Job thought he was okay before God.

The prophet Isaiah thought he was fine too—until he saw God in the temple (Isaiah 6). And Peter was fine as long as he was fishing. But when he saw Jesus, no longer was he fine (Luke 5). Likewise, when Job had an awesome revelation of God, he could only fall on his face and repent.

When we read Job 42, we finally see the full reward of Job's patience. Job's patience during his painful trial is only the first part of the story. The rest comes when his patience paid off in a new view of God and a new view of himself. Job learned that he needed God desperately and that he needed to decrease in his own life so God could increase. That is the heart of Job's lesson.

We can learn of God's compassion and mercy in the way God restored Job's fortunes. Most people want to camp there because they read that Job had more at the end of his life than he had at the start—and Job was a very wealthy man when this setback began. But there's more to Job's wealth than just simple reward. God gave him more possessions and a bigger bank account because Job found a new view of God and a new view of himself, and once that happened, God knew He could trust Job with more.

Job's wealth came because of his spiritual life, not because he named it and claimed it. God is not in the "stuff" business. Anyone who wants the kind of wealth Job had needs to be ready to endure as Job endured. But most of us don't want that deal, do we? Comfort is often more important to us than character, convenience more important than commitment, and cash more important than Christ. But God wants to turn that attitude on its head, and He will try us until we get things in proper perspective.

The Evidence of Patience

Now that we know something of the essence of patience and we've seen some examples of patience, let's talk about the evidence of patience—how we can tell when it is operating in our lives and setting us up for a comeback.

James gives us this important word about patience: "Above all, my brethren, do not swear, either by heaven or by earth or with any other oath; but your yes is to be yes, and your no, no, so that you may not fall under judgment" (James 5:12).

This statement comes on the heels of a discussion about the trials God sends our way to teach us patience and help us grow into mature Christians. But what do trials and patience have to do with making vows and swearing? The connection is clearer than you might think.

When you're in the midst of a painful trial, are you ever tempted to make promises you don't mean to keep? Do you find yourself praying, "Lord, if You'll get me out of this mess, I'll serve You the rest of my life," or "Lord, if You'll raise me up from this sickbed, I'll go anywhere You want."

Of course there is nothing wrong with making commitments to God. But promises from the foxhole usually don't stick. Almost every soldier under fire has made a rash promise to God. If God held us to all the promises we have made, I wouldn't be here to write this book, and you probably wouldn't be here to read it.

James says that if you exercise godly patience in your trial, you won't make all kinds of rash vows because you won't be so impatient to get things over with. Jesus also said special vows aren't necessary for those whose word is trustworthy (Matthew 5:33-37). He wasn't referring to oaths like those you make in a courtroom before testifying (although some people apply it that way), and neither was James. Jesus's focus, and that of James, was on our everyday conversation.

When you invoke God's name or swear by heaven, His throne, you are trying to obligate God to do things He may feel no obligation to perform. When you swear by heaven, you are out of bounds because you have no authority there. So you say, "Well, I'll swear by the earth." But the earth was created by God; it's His footstool, and you can't make things happen down here either.

Jesus told the leaders of His day not to swear even by themselves, because human beings don't have control over their own bodies, much less anything else. The point? Don't say anything that God can't or won't back up.

Peter got in trouble after making a rash vow: "Peter said to [Jesus], 'Even though all may fall away because of You, I will never fall away'" (Matthew 26:33). Peter was serious. He was sincere. But he made a vow he was not qualified to make. Peter not only broke his oath and denied Jesus, he used another form of oath taking when he cursed and swore and said he never knew Jesus. Do you know why Peter cursed? To add emphasis to his lie (Matthew 26:69-75).

That's why people who regularly use profanity to punctuate their speech can't be trusted. The same warning applies when someone has to add, "I swear to God" or "I swear it's the truth." If a person is speaking the truth, why does he have to add profanity or oaths to his words?

If you are a person of integrity, you don't need to add anything to give your words more weight. That's what Jesus meant when

He said, "Let your statement be, 'Yes, yes' or 'No, no'" (Matthew 5:37). James picked up on Jesus's teaching.

When you are experiencing a trial, that is not the time to start making worthless, impatient promises to God. And it's definitely not the time to curse your circumstances, the people around you, or your setback. When you squeeze a lemon or any piece of fruit, what do you get? You get whatever is inside. And when you squeeze a believer by putting him or her in a setback situation, what do you get? Whatever is inside. When God squeezes a believer, He wants to see what comes out. Does worship come out? What about prayer or praise? The Bible tells us to strengthen our hearts so when we are in the squeeze of a setback, what comes out is the righteousness we have built up inside.

The Rewards of Patience

I want to close with an encouraging word for you: Godly patience brings great reward. Jesus wasn't in Bethany when He got word that His friend Lazarus was sick, and He waited two days before going to the village. He arrived after Lazarus had died and been buried. Understandably, Mary and Martha wondered why in the world He had not come earlier and saved their brother, sparing the family a painful trial of heartache and loss. But Jesus had delayed His coming on purpose (John 11).

Do you ever feel as if you are about to die in your setback—and yet God has delayed His coming to you? Know that His occasional delays are always for a greater purpose. He wants us to develop patience, and when He doesn't come right away, we (like Mary and Martha) have no choice but to wait.

God may delay His arrival—He may leave us in our setback longer than we think is necessary—to help us develop patience. But here's the payoff, the reward for patience: The longer God leaves you in a setback situation when you are doing the best you can to be faithful, the greater the reward will be at the end. In other words, the longer the spiritual growing season, the greater the harvest at the end.

You see, if God bails you out of your setback too soon, the spiritual fruit He is growing in you will be underdeveloped. He knows just the right amount of time required to produce the greatest harvest.

A popular bumper sticker reads, "When the going gets tough, the tough go shopping." That's what a lot of Christians do. When the going gets tough, they say, "Let me out of here. Take me to the mall. Let me get this trial off my mind."

What we need to do when the going gets tough is go to our knees and say, "Lord, I'm waiting on You because I want the harvest of patience You are producing in my soul. I'm not going to make rash promises and swear and curse. I'm going to strengthen my heart so that what comes out of my mouth and heart honors You."

You may say, "But, Tony, I don't know what to do. I'm trying to hang in there, trying to wait for the Lord. But I'm running out of strength." God has something good for you. Isaiah 40 shares a prophecy about the Israelites returning from exile. The Jews were on their way back home, but they didn't know how they were going to make the long trip. So they complained, "My way is hidden from the LORD, and the justice due me escapes the notice of my God" (verse 27).

But the prophet answers, "Do you not know? Have you not heard? The Everlasting God, the LORD, the Creator of the ends of the earth does not become weary or tired. His understanding is inscrutable" (verse 28).

Here's what this great, powerful, limitless, beyond-our-understanding God does for those who wait patiently for Him:

> He gives strength to the weary, and to him who lacks might He increases power. Though youths grow weary and tired, and vigorous young men stumble badly, yet those who wait for the LORD will gain new strength; they will mount up with wings like eagles, they will run and not get tired, they will walk and not become weary (verses 29-31).

These words are sweet! God offers three levels of help for those who look to Him and wait for Him. I call them His intervention, His interaction, and His inner action. Eagles' wings represent God's intervention, when He swoops down to supernaturally intervene in your circumstances and bear you up. Eagles' wings may bring you the job you need, the mate you've been praying for, or the deliverance you seek.

When God runs with you so you don't get tired, that's His interaction. You're running along, wondering where your strength is corning from. Maybe you're running the race of the Christian life as a single person, and you're doing fine. God is running with you, talking with you along the way, saying, "Keep going. You're going to make it."

But sometimes you're tired, and you can't run anymore. God has something for you in those times too. He will slow down and walk with you so you don't become weary. This is God's inner action, in which He comes to your spirit, puts His arm around you, and says, "I know you're tired. You've been running for Jesus a long time. Let's just walk for a while."

He builds up your inner strength even when you feel weak. God becomes your spiritual walking stick, sustaining you even though your heart is weary.

Whatever your need may be, in each case God brings new strength. So if you are in a setback right now, be patient. Wait for the Lord, and He will renew your strength. And when the comeback has arrived, you'll see how far He's brought you all along.

Reflection and Application Questions

1. In this chapter, Tony shares with us the literal meaning of the Greek word translated "patience." Look back and find that interpretation, and describe what that kind of patience looks like in an everyday situation.

2. Scripture uses the analogy of a farmer growing food in the soil to describe patience at work.

   a. Why is it necessary for the seed to have time to germinate and grow in the process of farming? What would happen if, after the farmer planted the seed, she dug it up?

b. What other elements are needed (besides time) for that seed to germinate and produce what it is meant to produce?

c. Compare this illustration to patience in your own life. Does patience come simply through the passage of time? What other elements are needed for patience to produce the virtues and character qualities of godliness?

d. Describe some weeds that choke out the growth produced in patience (such as pride, anger, jealousy, or bitterness).

e. Identify any weeds in your own life that need to be uprooted so patience can have its full effect in your life. Write these down and ask the Lord to help you eliminate them.

3. According to this chapter, is being patient being passive?

a. Describe why or why not.

b. Look for places in your setback where you have been too passive. Write down ways you can take part in your own spiritual growth and comeback during your period of patience.

4. Read James 5:8. Commit this Scripture to memory. What does it mean to "strengthen your heart"? List three things you can do to help strengthen your heart while you are moving toward your comeback.

5. Galatians 5 lists the fruit of the Spirit: love, joy, peace, patience, kindness, goodness, faithfulness, gentleness, and self-control. Consider the importance of each one of these virtues in connection with patience. When we are impatient, we actually hinder our testimony of reflecting Jesus Christ to those around us. When we are patient, we shine a light that shows others the Holy Spirit's residence and authority in our lives. Describe a practical way you can integrate each of these fruits of the Spirit into your specific setback situation:

a. Love

b. Joy

c. Peace

d. Patience

e. Kindness

f. Goodness

g. Faithfulness

h. Gentleness

i. Self-control

9

ACCEPT DIRECTION

I wasn't allowed to attend many movies when I was growing up, but I do remember seeing old 3-D movies. We were given a pair of glasses that made the images on the screen really come alive. To see what was going on, you had to wear those glasses. If you didn't, something like a haze seemed to hang over the screen, and you could hardly tell what was happening. But when you put on the 3-D glasses, not only could you see clearly, but the action seemed to fly off the screen and jump right into your lap.

On your way toward your comeback, you will need to put on a pair of spiritual 3-D glasses and see life in an entirely new dimension. More specifically, when you put on your "Holy Spirit glasses" and look at life from God's perspective, things start falling into place and making sense.

Seeing in God's spiritual 3-D is an exciting way to live, just as watching a 3-D movie was an exciting way to spend a Saturday afternoon. How do you see in 3-D? As you prepare to go after your comeback, you plan your life in complete dependence upon God. Your plans need to reflect God's character and His will for you. Unless you plan with your Holy Spirit glasses on, life is going to be hazy and unclear. You won't know what your next move should be. So let's explore how life looks when we view it from God's perspective.

Submit to God's Sovereignty As You Plan

The starting point for all our planning and the foundation of your comeback is recognition of God's sovereignty. With that acknowledgment, you say that God is in control and you aren't. Making plans without submitting them for His review, correction, and approval is an act of arrogance that God will not let go unchallenged. As the apostle James put it, "Come now, you who say, 'Today or tomorrow we will go to such and such a city, and spend a year there and engage in business and make a profit'" (James 4:13).

"Hold on a minute," he seems to say. "Did you ask God? Did He get to vote?"

Making decisions and plans without God reflects a worldview without God. We can also call this "worldly." It's no surprise, then, that lost people act in a worldly manner, because they don't know life with God. But a "worldly Christian" is an oxymoron, a contradiction. Yet it is also a reality. The Bible helps believers see our own worldliness by inviting us to consider how we approach the everyday details of life. In today's language, God is saying, "Get real! Don't give Me that stuff about you not being worldly when you exclude Me from your plans."

Do you see the arrogance in the statement from James 4:13?

Do you see any room for God to lead or even to offer an opinion? This finite human is making fixed, airtight plans as if he or she has total control over every detail of life, but the truth is that we can't control anything—especially our own comeback.

We are dependent by nature—dependent on circumstances, people, and of course, God. God, on the other hand, is totally independent by nature. He will do what He wants to do. God's plans are not contingent upon anything else. We might make plans to fly to a certain city on a certain day and take care of some business. But those plans depend on the airlines, the weather, the business climate, and many other things we can't control.

Whenever we make plans, we assume we will wake up tomorrow with our bodies in working order. We assume the transportation we need will be available.

I know life calls for us to make plans. I actually have to "plan" my schedule a year or more in advance. But there are too many uncertainties and unknowns between now and next year for me to say confidently, "This is what I am going to do—period." I am not independent, and neither are you.

Of course, God does not condemn human planning. The Bible urges us to plan (Proverbs 6:6-8). But God is the Author of the eternal timetable. And your comeback isn't about to happen in a way that you can plan. Only God knows all the moving pieces that must come together at precisely the right time for it to come about.

The Danger of Excluding God

Again, it's not sinful to plan. In fact, it's unwise not to plan. We are to be good stewards of the life God has given us. But God does condemn independent planning that leaves Him out, and schedule-making that does not allow for His engagement. These plans will never succeed.

Making plans without God is like hacking through a jungle without a map or being at sea without a compass—you'll wind up lost. It's like playing a football game with no preparation—you'll lose. Without God, your plans will fall apart; you'll have nothing to show for your efforts.

My oldest daughter, Crystal, loves puzzles. When she was a child, she always wanted a puzzle for Christmas. As Crystal grew older, I bought her more complex puzzles. One year I bought her a 1,000-piece puzzle for Christmas. She took the puzzle back to her bedroom, joyfully anticipating the challenge ahead of her. But after spending the better part of the day in her room, Crystal came out angry. She was irritated with me. She wanted to know why I had bought her that puzzle.

I asked her, "What's the problem?"

She came back with a classic answer: "Dad, this puzzle has too many pieces."

That's true of life too. It has too many pieces. No matter how smart you are, you can't put this puzzle together without help. That's why puzzle makers put a picture on the box lid. As long as you get help from the puzzle maker, you can put the pieces together. But you can't force a piece to fit where the puzzle maker didn't design it to fit.

James 4:13-17 makes clear that to plan your business, your travel, or your day-to-day life without including God is a sign of worldliness—and it is sinful. It's not enough to acknowledge God on Sunday morning. He must be part of the totality of existence.

When something happens that you didn't anticipate—and it will—chances are that you won't know how to handle it if you haven't allowed a place in your plans for God's activity.

Too many Christians have handed God their Declaration of Independence. Like the devil, they are telling God, "I will, I will, I will. These are my plans, God, and I'm going to make them happen." That's planning for disaster. We need to do our planning in dependence on God's sovereign direction.

We can also plan with His infinite knowledge in mind. After all, He knows the end from the beginning. The Bible reminds us that we are human beings: "Yet you do not know what your life will be like tomorrow. You are just a vapor that appears for a little while and then vanishes away" (James 4:14). Our knowledge—like our life—is limited. How could we, then, plan a comeback if we don't even have the capacity to plan for tomorrow with any degree of certainty?

You and I don't even know what tomorrow holds, Scripture tells us, so why are we talking so confidently about what we will and will not do? Words like that betray our worldliness and lack of humility. It's easy to demonstrate just how limited our knowledge is. Don't all of us make plans only to be disappointed when something unforeseen happens?

Remember when you thought you were going to get that raise or promotion? Confident that it was coming, you might have gone out and bought stuff before the raise actually came through, but for some reason, it didn't.

Or perhaps you thought everything at the Realtor's office was moving along well and the new house was going to be yours. Or you thought you would be able to afford the new car payment, but then something in the house broke and now you're strapped. How did you get into that mess? Because you're not God, and you can't see what's coming next.

In Psalm 73, the psalmist was shaken when he looked around and noticed that evil people seemed to have everything going their way. They grew rich and fat and never had trouble, while the righteous went from problem to problem. So the psalmist pointed out this apparent injustice to the Lord. When he did, God showed him the real deal, which is essentially that the wicked have one foot on a banana peel and the other foot in hell.

When the psalmist saw things as they really are, when he put on his "Holy Ghost glasses," he said he felt "senseless and ignorant…like a beast before [God]" (verse 22). We would say today that he did a facepalm and said, "OMG!"

We are indeed like senseless animals when it comes to advising God on how to run His universe. You don't go to your pet for advice on how you should conduct your life, and God doesn't come to us. Again, the best proof of our limited knowledge is that we don't even know what's going to happen tomorrow. That's why Scripture tells us, "Do not boast about tomorrow, for you do not know what a day may bring forth" (Proverbs 27:1). In fact, we can't even be sure we are going to make it through today. The emergency room is full of people who had plans for later.

We lean on God's infinite knowledge, first, because our knowledge is limited, and second, because our days are limited. "Life is short," they say. You hear it a lot because it's true. And the older you get, the faster time moves.

When you're a child, time creeps along. "Why is it taking so long to become a teenager?" you ask. When you finally become a teenager, time starts to walk a little bit. You can see the day ahead when you will leave the house and go to college or work. When you become an adult, time starts to run. Life is going by faster. Then when you are older, time just flies. You wonder where it went. And you can see the day when your time on this planet will run out.

We use terms such as "young" and "old" to describe people's ages, but these terms are relative because we don't know how long our lives will be. But one thing is sure—our lives are just a vapor, a puff of smoke, because God measures our days against eternity.

We must include God in the thoughts and plans of life, and especially related to a comeback, because He knows what we don't know. He sees every factor, takes into consideration all possibilities, and gives us the best option.

Let me compare this to an everyday situation. If you live in a city that broadcasts regular traffic reports on the radio, you know what it's like to want to go somewhere and wonder if traffic will block your way. When I need to get across Dallas, I tune in to a local station that has a helicopter in the air checking on traffic. Why? My knowledge of the current traffic situation is extremely limited. I don't know if traffic is backed up just around the corner. I don't know if there has been an accident on my route, because I can't see any farther than a few feet in front of my car.

But the radio station can help me because it has an "eye in the sky" that can take in the traffic scene all at once. The pilot can suggest an alternate route if my original route is stacked up. (You may think this is an old illustration because you probably use a GPS—but I have not migrated to a GPS just yet, so the helicopter will have to do!)

As you navigate your way through life, you are low, but God is high. He can see all the possible routes, and He can show you the one that can keep you out of a mess. But God will share His infinite knowledge with you only if you "switch on your radio" and include Him in your planning. Because life is so short—and we are so finite in our knowledge—we can't afford to exclude Him. If you need a comeback, you don't have time to waste.

The writers of Scripture also knew that life is short, and they were faithful to remind us.

"Our days on the earth are like a shadow" (1 Chronicles 29:15).

"My days are swifter than a weaver's shuttle" (Job 7:6).

"Teach us to number our days" (Psalm 90:12).

All of us have made decisions without God's direction. If given the opportunity to turn back the clock, we would undoubtedly do things differently. Hindsight is always better than foresight. The bad news is, we can't go back. Time is like a coin. You can spend it any way you want, but you can only spend it once.

But the good news is you're still alive, and that means you still have the opportunity to make better and wiser decisions today. You can't change yesterday, but today doesn't have to look like yesterday if you plan in dependence on God's perfect knowledge.

Defer to God's Will As You Plan

The saints of the past used to finish their sentences by saying, "Lord willing." They also went to church and sang praises that God had brought them safely through another week. They understood something many of us have forgotten today. Perhaps because life was harsher and more uncertain in those days, God's people in earlier generations learned to say, "If the Lord wills, we will live and also do this or that" (James 4:15). This is something all of us ought to say.

With our limited knowledge and limited life spans, we are wise to defer to God's will when we are making plans. We do well to punctuate our pronouncements about the future with a spiritual proviso. But saying "If the Lord wills" should be far more than just a phrase to make you sound spiritual. These words need to reflect an attitude that says, "Lord, these are my plans, but I subject them to Your will because You are infinitely greater than I am." That attitude includes God in your planning.

Since God's will for you is the expression of His infinitely perfect plan, you can't go wrong submitting your plans to Him. But if you leave God out, you may miss out on the comeback He is trying to send your way. You may also miss out on His protection from some danger if you are fixated on what you want to do.

Have you ever met people who are rigid and inflexible? They're tough to deal with because their plans leave no room for anyone else's will—even God's. Jesus said, "My food is to do the will of Him who sent Me" (John 4:34). Doing God's will was as satisfying to Jesus as a good meal is to most of us. When you include God's will in your planning, you know God's satisfaction. And His will is so satisfying because it is "good and acceptable and perfect" (Romans 12:2).

God's will satisfies, and that is good news for those of us who desire to obey God. And here is more good news—God wants us to know and understand His will. He wants us to test and prove His will, and He wants us to obey His will. For example, because of the intimate relationship God had with Moses, God "made known His ways to Moses" (Psalm 103:7). If you have a growing, intimate relationship with God, He will let you in on what He's doing with your life.

But if your relationship with God is shaky because you're an SMO (Sunday Morning Only) Christian or because you won't let God into your business or your family life, then He will say, "Fine. Do it on your own."

Honor God's Holiness As You Plan

This final point takes us right to the heart of the planning issue. Our plans are not just a matter of intelligence or convenience, but a matter of holiness. To plan apart from God is sin. The Bible says, "As it is, you boast in your arrogance; all such boasting is evil. Therefore, to one who knows the right thing to do and does not do it, to him it is sin" (James 4:16-17). As always, God is clear. God-less planning is not just bad planning. It's sinful, unholy planning. We insult the character of God when we deliberately exclude Him from our lives.

God is distinct from His creation. This is one of the fundamental truths of Scripture. He is with us, He is close to us, but there is a dividing line between Him and us, much like the line between parents and children. Parents don't always tell their children everything. They reserve the right to keep some of their plans and intentions private. In those cases, when children ask why, the parent doesn't say much. Other times, parents explain things more fully to their children.

Likewise, God reserves His right as Creator to step into our lives and ask us to obey even when we don't understand exactly what is going on. But because He is perfect, holy, and loving, we can trust Him.

The people to whom this passage was addressed were not just being worldly in their planning; they were bragging about their independence from God. The word "boast" here suggests a peddler trying to sell something.

You may remember the peddlers in the old Westerns who pulled into town in their wagons, opened the side of the wagon, and started selling elixirs they claimed could cure any illness. It was pure chicanery. The peddler was giving people the impression that his potion could do things it wasn't really capable of doing.

That's what happens when people brag about how they don't need God. They give the impression they can do things they really can't do. And that's evil. God says,

> Let not a wise man boast of his wisdom, and let not the mighty man boast of his might, let not a rich man boast of his riches; but let him who boasts boast of this, that he understands and knows Me, that I am the Lord who exercises lovingkindness, justice and righteousness on earth; for I delight in these things (Jeremiah 9:23-24).

In other words, don't brag that you have a lot of money; God can take it away from you in a heartbeat. Don't brag about your degrees; they may only be good as wall decorations. Don't brag because you work out at the gym; you can get hit with a cold that will put you in bed for a week.

If you want to brag, tell people that you know God. Brag about Him, not about the great plans you have made. That is sheer pride. Furthermore, this kind of boasting leads to spiritual rebellion, and that leads to sin. Sin is more than just doing something wrong. We sin when we know what is right and yet fail to do it.

The tragic story of the ocean liner *Titanic* is a classic example of the boastful arrogance that leads to disaster. The people who put that ship in the water were convinced it was unsinkable. The company that owned the *Titanic* was so confident about its seaworthiness that they built extra passenger rooms in the space that should have been used for lifeboats. Advertisements for the *Titanic* boasted of its safety. One passenger, however, told her husband she didn't want to sail on the *Titanic* because she believed the owners were tempting God by bragging that their ship could never sink.

Jesus told a story that offers an even better example of prideful planning. It's the story of the foolish farmer:

> The land of a rich man was very productive. And he began reasoning to himself, saying, "What shall I do, since I have no place to store my crops?" Then he said, "This is what I will do: I will tear down my barns and build larger ones, and there I will store all my grain and my goods. And I will say to my soul, 'Soul, you have many goods laid up for many years to come; take your ease, eat, drink and be merry'" (Luke 12:16-19).

This guy sounds like an investor on a television infomercial—one of those people who have their investments all made and secured and are looking forward to retirement. They already know where they are going to retire, and how they are going to play golf, travel, and do all the things they've always wanted to do.

Again, God is not against our planning for the future. He is not offended when we dream. But—as we have been saying all along—just don't leave God out of your plans. Or worse, don't wave your plans around as if to say to God, "Here's what I plan to do in order to get my comeback, and You can't stop me."

The farmer Jesus talked about was a fool because God was nowhere in his thoughts or plans. And God said to him, "You fool! This very night your soul is required of you" (verse 20). The party was over before it started for him.

This farmer must have been in good health, because he clearly figured he had many years left. He also thought he had the money to enjoy his retirement. But he died utterly broke spiritually and financially. And everyone dies broke financially. No matter how much money you have when you die, you leave it all behind, and it belongs to somebody else. So you are penniless when you leave this life.

If the foolish farmer in Jesus's parable had put his faith in God, he could have left this world as a fabulously rich person with all the wealth of heaven at his disposal. And that was Jesus's point: "So is the man who stores up treasure for himself, and is not rich toward God" (verse 21).

This man told himself, "I'm going to live a long time." God said, "You fool, today is your last day on planet earth." Wouldn't a person be a fool to plan with certainty for the next 30 years without considering that he might not make it through the night?

The farmer had success, satisfaction, and security. But Jesus saw him as a man facing death. The man had decided how well off he was spiritually by looking at what he had accumulated materially. The farmer looked at his barns but started talking to his soul.

You may look at your bank account and start talking to your body. You may say, "Body, today you are going to wear designer clothes and diamond jewelry. You are going to drive the finest car available and live in a palatial home." But you can't look at your bank account and tell your soul that it is well off. The foolish farmer spent his life on himself, but he never made any investments for his soul.

I don't believe you want to make foolish plans for your life. Don't let prideful planning push you away from your comeback. Make plans, yes—but do so in submission to God's sovereignty, relying on His infinite knowledge, deferring to His will, and honoring His holiness.

Reflection and Application Questions

1. Tony opens this chapter with an illustration on watching 3-D movies; 3-D glasses let us see the movie in a more complete way. He connects this to what the Holy Spirit does in our lives when He gives us insight and direction on the spiritual aspects of life, making the picture clearer. Often God works behind the scenes and in ways we cannot readily see. Discovering His direction and then applying that direction to our decisions requires spiritual sensitivity and faith. Read 2 Kings 6:17-18. Compare and contrast what Elisha prayed regarding his friend and his enemy.

    a. How did God respond to Elisha's request?

    b. In what way does opening your own eyes to see from a spiritual vantage point give you direction in life?

    c. Do you regularly pray and ask God to help you see the spiritual realm operating behind the physical realm? How can you commit to making that part of your daily prayer life?

2. Read James 4:13. Compare this verse to Proverbs 3:6. Which approach to life will yield the best potential outcome, and why?

3. Tony shares with us that planning our days and decisions without including God is a form of worldliness and is sinful. List some ways you make plans that do not include God's viewpoint. How can you include God's direction in these plans in the future?

4. Read and memorize 1 Chronicles 29:15, Job 7:6, and Psalm 90:12. What insight do you receive from these three verses? In what ways do they encourage you to live life more intentionally, seeking God's purposes and plans for your life?

5. In Luke 12, Jesus told the story of a wealthy farmer. This farmer was successful according to the world's standards. In fact, he was so successful that he decided to tear down his barns and storage units and build larger ones in which to place his worldly goods. What did he plan to do once he built the larger storage units?

a. What happened to this wealthy farmer instead?

b. How important is it to function from a spiritual standpoint rather than in worldly wisdom?

c. In what ways can you incorporate God's wisdom and direction at a greater level in your own personal decisions and planning?

10

PURSUE GREATER INTIMACY

When we are facing a setback, one of the most natural things to do is to seek a way out of it. We search for our comeback. But it's wiser to pursue God, because your comeback is found in God alone. The believer who is focused on drawing closer to God won't have to worry very much about finding their comeback or God's plan for their lives. When you find the One who holds both of these in His hands, you'll find what you're looking for.

As you face any setback in life, make it your goal to pursue a deeper, more intimate relationship with God right where He has put you. Let's talk about three ways the Bible says you can do this.

Submit to God

First, submit to God's authority in your life. Scripture tells us, "Submit therefore to God" (James 4:7). That's about as clear as it gets.

But what does the "therefore" point back to? In the verses preceding this one, you'll find a discussion of the value God places on humility. An attitude of humility before God is the key to submitting ourselves to Him. A person with a me-focused, proud spirit isn't about to submit to anyone—not even God.

Submission has never been a popular concept. This is particularly true in our social-media saturated, me-crazed society. But you can't skip it if you want to pursue God fully. As you will see, God has a lot of benefits and blessings in store for the believer who is fully submitted to Him.

This principle of submission appears throughout the Bible. We are commanded to submit to duly constituted government (Romans 13:1). A wife is to submit herself to the legitimate authority of her husband (Ephesians 5:22), and children are instructed to obey their parents (Ephesians 6:1).

Of course there are exceptions, as when an authority may tell us to do something directly contrary to God's Word. But submission to authority is the rule. "Submission" is a military term meaning "placing yourself in your proper rank." It means to place yourself under the authorities God has put over you and, ultimately, to position yourself under His authority. We could say, then, that submission to God requires a new alignment of our lives.

When your tires are out of alignment, you may feel your car pull to one side. Sometimes you can't detect the problem while driving, but you can know your car needs an alignment when the front tires begin to wear unevenly.

Some Christians look at their lives and see the uneven wear. They may even feel themselves being pulled to one side or the other by the world, the flesh, and the devil. They may be experiencing more defeats than victories. They find themselves unable to cope with the constant battle with sin that believers must fight every day. They know there's a problem, so they keep changing "tires," hoping to solve it. Let me explain.

Christians who don't feel fully aligned with the Lord may keep changing churches, hoping to find something that can pull them back in proper alignment with God. Or they may go after a certain spiritual experience that promises something new, running from conference to seminar in search of help.

But if the front end of your car is out of alignment, changing tires won't fix it; the new tires will simply begin to wear out like the old ones. The same is true spiritually. You can change your spiritual tires every week, but that won't help unless you submit your life to God on a daily basis. Until you bring your heart into its proper alignment under God's authority, you are still going to wear out as you face whatever setback life gives you.

Submission to God means saying to Him day by day, "Not my will, but Your will be done. I subject my desires to Your desires, my dreams to Your dreams, my purposes and plans to Your purposes and plans." It's utterly abandoning yourself to God's control.

If you've been aligned with the world, taking your orders from the culture and from your old sinful nature, you'll find it tough to get yourself back in rank under your Commander, Jesus Christ. But this is a necessary first step to being in a right relationship with God and experiencing a comeback.

Here's another way to think about submission. Imagine you're in bed on a dark, cold winter morning, comfortable in the spot you have warmed up, and you hear the alarm go off. You know what that means. It's time to get up. But that spot in your bed is so warm and comfortable. You don't want to leave your bed and put your feet on a cold floor.

But you get up anyway. You choose to get out of bed and prepare for your day. Why? Because you know that the rewards of going to work or caring for your family, of earning a living so you can provide the house that holds your warm bed or take care of those within it, are greater than the temporary pleasure of a few extra minutes in a warm bed. You may not feel like getting up on that particular morning. But the price for turning over and staying in bed is too high to pay.

Submitting to God requires the choice (an act of the will) to leave that little warm spot we have developed in the world. God is calling us to leave our temporary comfort for the greater reward of getting ourselves in proper rank under Him. God can empower you to make that decision, but He will not make it for you. Submission to God involves a conscious decision to throw back the covers of a lesser, temporary comfort and seek the greater blessing of intimacy with God. Through that, you will find the ability to come back.

Resist the Devil

Like a magnet with positive and negative poles, submission to God also has a negative pole: "Submit therefore to God. Resist the devil and he will flee from you" (James 4:7). Drawing closer to God will help you resist Satan's attempt to influence you. Remember, Satan has no power over you that you don't allow him to have. The devil is not invincible. He has been "render[ed] powerless" by the death of Jesus Christ (Hebrews 2:14).

Because the devil cannot overcome us by power, he has to attack us with deception and temptation. Satan can make you want to sin, but if you are a believer, Satan can no longer make you sin. He simply makes sin look attractive and easy for you to commit.

The devil is smart. He doesn't waste his time tempting us in areas where we are not vulnerable. He is a student of our lives. He has a game film on us, and he studies it like a football coach who wants to know his opponent's habits, tendencies, and preferences. Satan's film on your life goes all the way back to your unsaved days. He and his demons have studied that tape so long that they know what you like to do, what you like to think about, the places you like to go, and the people you like to hang out with.

Knowing all this, the devil's strategy is to present you with circumstances and people that will bring out your sinful tendencies. When you see how the devil has lined up against you, draw on the power of Jesus Christ and call a new play at the line of scrimmage. You change the play so the devil's knowledge of your tendencies and weak spots does not give him the power to control your thoughts and actions.

Our greatest example of resisting the devil comes from Jesus Christ. In Satan's temptation of Jesus, we find the keys to resisting Satan in our lives.

We first read, "Jesus was led up by the Spirit into the wilderness to be tempted by the devil" (Matthew 4:1). Notice that this temptation was on God's terms, not the devil's. God opened the door to this opportunity, and Jesus Christ confronted the devil head-on. Of course, we shouldn't go looking for the devil, but we need to remember that Satan can attack us only on God's terms. The devil can't go any further than God allows him to go.

Next we see that Jesus did not take the devil's temptation lightly. Jesus "fasted forty days and forty nights" in spiritual preparation (verse 2). Even Jesus, God in the flesh, did not meet the devil without being prepared. He spent a lot of time preparing in His Father's presence, an example of perfect submission to God.

This point is critical. You can't resist the devil if your spiritual immune system is weak. When your body's immune system is weak, you become vulnerable to illness. Your resistance—spiritual and physical—becomes low when you don't have enough disease fighters in your system.

What does it take to keep your spiritual resistance high? Jesus fasted and prayed. He sacrificed bodily comfort for spiritual strength. If you have little desire for spiritual things, if you are making few or no sacrifices of creature comforts in the pursuit of God, your spiritual resistance will be low. And Satan knows when you are weak. In that case, even though you may tell him to leave, he won't budge because he knows you don't have enough strength and energy to resist him.

The devil cannot hurt or defeat the believer whose immune system is strong because that person is living in submission to God. But if you are living in perpetual spiritual defeat, your resistance is down. Your spiritual immune system is deficient in the basics that keep a believer strong against Satan. When you submit to God, you find the strength you need to resist the devil. Jesus may have been physically weak, but He was spiritually strong after 40 days of preparation. You can read the account of His temptation in Matthew 4:3-11.

Notice that first, the devil acted in character. He tempted Jesus to act independently of God and create food, put on a show, and take the kingdom apart from God's will. But Jesus defeated the devil at each turn by quoting the Word: "It is written" (verses 4,7,10). Jesus used the Word of God, the one thing that gets past the devil's immune system.

You see, the devil has an immune system too. He can handle all our promises and resolutions to do better and our attempts to resist him in our own strength. But the Word of God always takes the devil down. Obviously, then, to resist the devil, you need to know your Bible. That means being so thoroughly immersed in the truth of Scripture that you can quote it on the spot to ward off the devil's attacks.

After Jesus had hit the devil three times with the Word, the devil's resistance was so low he had nothing left to fight with, and he left. He couldn't function in that environment. So instead of letting the devil weaken our immune systems and make us sick, we should be making him sick by submitting to God and growing skilled in the Word. We should be learning and memorizing the Word, not so we can impress others and win Bible quoting contests, but so we can win at life.

———

I recently ministered at a treatment center in New Jersey that offers the most phenomenal recovery program I've ever seen. When men with addictions go there for two weeks, they have to sign an agreement to abide by the rules of the program, which are very strict. This program saturates people with the Word of God. The men who enter the program have to read the Word, quote it, memorize it, and study it. The idea is to help them increase their resistance and build up their spiritual immune systems before they deal with the problems that have led to their addictions.

I was told that 80 percent of the men who go through the program leave in victory, and only 5 percent have to come back. When I commented on these great statistics, the director told me that the key is strengthening the spiritual immune system before trying to deal with the addiction. Otherwise, he said, the help is only temporary. But if they can show a man how to build up his spiritual strength, the effects of the other counseling are lasting.

Submitting to God will help you resist the devil. Resist him with prayer, spiritual discipline, and the Word, just as Jesus did, and the devil will have to leave. He cannot function in that environment.

Draw Near to God

There once was a little boy who was beaten up by a bully every day on his way to school. The boy's friends told him to go to school a different way. But the bully found out about that route, met the boy on his way to school, and beat him up.

Another friend advised the boy to carry a stick to school. He carried a stick one day, but the bully took the stick away from him and beat him with it. Nothing this boy tried worked. One day as the boy was walking to school, the bully jumped out and clenched his fist. But instead of being afraid, the boy said, "Come on, I'm ready. I'll take you right now."

The bully couldn't believe this little kid had become so brave. But as the bully got ready to pounce on him, the boy's father stepped out from behind a bush. He was about six feet five and 275 pounds. The bully said, "Uh-oh."

The moral of the story is, stay close to your Father. The closer you are to God, the more that bully the devil will leave you alone. That's why the Word of God tells us, "Draw near to God and He will draw near to you" (James 4:8). This is the second part of the Bible's formula for greater intimacy with God.

That intimacy is key if you are to grow into the believer God wants you to be. After all, you cannot avoid worldliness and beat the devil at his game if you're maintaining a long-distance relationship with God. You cannot be a part-time Christian, an SMO (Sunday Morning Only) saint, and still mature into the Christian God wants you to be.

The closer you draw to God, the more like Him you are going to become. You can't help being affected, the way you can't help sweating if you're out in the hot sun. Greater closeness to God gives you a greater likeness to Him.

But you don't draw close to someone by accident. You have to plan for closeness. Intentionality is necessary to achieve intimacy. It doesn't just happen.

If you are married, chances are good that you and your mate did not simply drift to the altar. You drew near to one another as you got acquainted and began to spend time together. You talked on the phone. You texted. You went out on dates. And when you weren't together, you wished you were. You began thinking about each other all the time. Your investment in nearness produced an intensity of relationship, which led to the altar.

Most marriages start off with a passionate intimacy, but what often happens as the years go by? It's easy for a couple to drift apart emotionally when they find themselves dealing with other agendas and looking after their children. If a married couple has no ongoing plan to draw near to one another, they will drift danger-ously apart. Then one day they look up and find that the marriage is weak and in trouble. It is inevitable. When you allow distance in any relationship to go on too long, the relationship dies.

Your relationship with God is a lot like a marriage relation-ship. Intimacy with Him won't happen by chance. You need to make an intentional commitment to pursue God and seek greater intimacy with Him so He can grow you into a greater likeness to Jesus Christ.

When we make that commitment, we have the tremendous promise that He will draw near to us. Just as in a good marriage, the commitment is not one-sided. God is eager to bring us near.

Someone might ask, "If God wants me closer, why doesn't He draw near to me, and then I'll draw near to Him? Why do I have to initiate the process?" The answer is simple. He's not the one who pulled back. He's not the one who left. That brings us to the issue of sin.

Deal Seriously with Sin

Suppose a man walks out on his family, gets his own apart-ment, establishes a separate life, and then says, "If my family will draw near to me, I'll draw near to them."

That's not right. He has it backward. He's the one who left home; it's his job to repent, return, and draw near to his family. It's the same in our relationship with God. Our sin breaks our fel-lowship with Him and puts distance between us. When we return to God in repentance, willing to change our ways, we'll find that He never left.

What does it take to draw near to God? The Bible answers in

no uncertain terms: "Cleanse your hands, you sinners; and purify your hearts, you double-minded" (James 4:8). Clearly, James is talking to Christians here, because non-Christians can't cleanse their hands and be clean. They first need a "whole-body" cleansing through the blood of Christ. James is addressing Christians who are living like sinners.

Why does James tell us to wash our hands? Hand washing was part of the cleansing ceremony that Old Testament priests performed before they could offer sacrifices to God. The act symbolized getting rid of the defilement of sin.

Hands represent our external actions, just as the heart represents our internal attitudes. Cleansing our hands means saying to God, "I know this is sin. I know it is defiling me, and I'm going to stop it." God wants us to make this decision to change any of our sinful actions.

But we are often reluctant to call sin what it is. We call it everything but sin: a weakness, a problem, a mistake, a bad choice, an issue. God will deal with you only if you are ready to deal openly and directly with your sin.

Dealing with sin means being cleansed and purified. It also means focusing on the Lord and His ways as opposed to being double-minded or unable to make up your mind about whether you want to line up with God or line up with the world. It means not wanting to be a saint and a sinner at the same time. That kind of spiritual indecision is deadly because God pulls back when He sees a believer who flops back and forth between commitment and compromise.

Some of us are double-minded when we hang around the edges of sin—just close enough to keep within reach. We don't really want to plunge into the dirtiness of sin. We just want to collect some of sin's souvenirs so we can put them in the attic and get them out every once in a while.

But God calls us to clean out the attic too. He wants us to get rid of the reminders of the world. He says, "Don't let your heart be divided." And He invites us to go to Him as David did when he said, "Against You, You only, I have sinned" (Psalm 51:4). When we remove the sin, God will be free to draw near.

We hear that promise throughout Scripture:

- The LORD is near to all who call upon Him, to all who call upon Him in truth" (Psalm 145:18).
- "You will seek Me and find Me when you search for Me with all your heart" (Jeremiah 29:13).
- "Draw near with confidence" (Hebrews 4:16).
- "Draw near with a sincere heart" (Hebrews 10:22).

In case we somehow miss the intensity of God's desire for us to deal with sin, James adds, "Be miserable and mourn and weep; let your laughter be turned into mourning and your joy to gloom" (James 4:9).

Doesn't it bother you when you're in a serious situation and somebody who should be taking it seriously laughs it off as if it were no big deal? God says, "Don't brush off sin as if it were nothing serious. It's serious." If you want to draw near to God, you have to adopt His attitude toward sin. Weep bitterly over your sin as Peter did when he denied Jesus three times (Matthew 26:69-75). Grieve and agonize over your sin as King David did (Psalm 51). He didn't blame his sinful deeds on his past or on someone else.

That's what it means to "be miserable and mourn and weep" over your sin. It's evidence of sincere repentance. If you don't think your sin is bad enough to cry over, if you're comparing your "little" sin to some of the really bad sins, you don't understand how God views sin. All sin is a deep affront to His holiness. We cannot enjoy nearness to God, real intimacy with Him, when sin is present. Sin never fails to choke off our fellowship with our Lord.

Humble Yourself Before God

The third step in this biblical formula for seeking God is this: "Humble yourselves in the presence of the Lord, and He will exalt you" (James 4:10). It's yet another great promise from the Word. If we are busy lifting ourselves up, why should God do any lifting? Humility means we go low so God can lift us high.

We know true humility when God has removed all fragments of pride from us. The people God lifted up in the Bible were always taken down first. Joseph was taken down to Egypt to become a slave and do time in prison before he became prime minister of the land (Genesis 39). Moses was sent out into the desert for 40 years before he was ready to lead Israel (Exodus 2). David had to hang out with the sheep and spend years running for his life before he could be king (1–2 Samuel). These people—and many others— had to learn humility before God trusted them with great positions and responsibilities.

If you want God to raise you up in usefulness, power, victory, and strength, you must go low. Why? Because there is no room for two Gods in this universe. If you raise yourself up to be God over your life, the true God will have no room to work. But if you can't raise yourself up and you realize you are in desperate need of God, you can go low before Him in humility.

When you need mercy, you say please. When you need grace, you ask humbly.

Then you will know a sweet intimacy with your Lord. Arrogant people don't know such intimacy or nearness to God. He does not invite the proud to draw close. So you must let go of all pride if you are to reach God's heart. His elevator to the top always starts by going down.

God's Word both tells us to humble ourselves and gives an illustration of what humility looks like in real life. Not surprisingly, one example addresses the way we use our tongues.

> Do not speak against one another, brethren. He who speaks against a brother or judges his brother, speaks against the law and judges the law; but if you judge the law, you are not a doer of the law but a judge of it (James 4:11).

Humbling yourself before God means, in part, never using your tongue to hurt other people and drag them down. That comes more easily when you acknowledge your own sin and shortcomings. Pride lets us exalt ourselves and treat other people with contempt. Humility lets us see that we are all on level ground before God. For that reason, attacks on a fellow believer have no place in the life of a Christian who is pursuing intimacy with God.

"Who are you who judge your neighbor?" the Bible asks (James 4:12). Put differently, how dare we tear down a brother or sister when we ourselves cannot stand before God because of our sin? If God started keeping accounts, none of us would be around long. Humility demands that we deal with our own shortcomings rather than look at other people's sin. Focusing on other people's failings can lead us to "speak against" them. To "speak against" a fellow Christian here means to slander the person, to speak viciously with the evil intent of destroying another person's reputation. The opposite of such slander is speech that is "good for edification according to the need of the moment, so that it will give grace to those who hear" (Ephesians 4:29).

Do you use your words to tear people down or to build them up? Your speech matters a great deal to God. Notice that slandering a fellow Christian is a violation of God's royal law, which says, "You shall love your neighbor as yourself" (James 2:8). No one wants to have his or her reputation destroyed! When we fail to exercise humility as we talk about others, we set ourselves above God's law and treat it with contempt. That is a very dangerous thing to do.

Jesus summarized all of God's law by saying we should love God with our whole being and our neighbor as ourselves (Matthew 22:37-40). The Ten Commandments are really about love (Exodus 20:3-17). Let me show you.

The first commandment forbids another God: Our love can't be fickle; it must be single-minded. The second commandment forbids idols: Love must be loyal. The third commandment forbids taking God's name in vain: Love must be respectful. The fourth commandment tells us to remember the Sabbath and keep it holy: Love must be focused in its affections.

The next six commandments address our relationships with others. The fifth commandment tells us to honor our father and mother: Love must be submissive to legitimate authority. The sixth commandment forbids murder: Love values other people. The seventh commandment rules out adultery: Marital love is to be pure, undefiled, and loyal.

The eighth commandment forbids stealing: Love is not to be selfish and take from others what belongs to them. The ninth commandment tells us not to bear false witness: Love must be truthful. And the tenth commandment forbids coveting: Love must be content and thankful.

Clearly, love is built into the Ten Commandments. Therefore love must govern the way we talk about others. The person who tears down a brother or sister breaks God's law.

Yet the Bible does not say we can never assess other people's trustworthiness. At times, judgment is appropriate and even necessary for that person's spiritual well-being. The key is the attitude with which we make our judgments. Again, the Bible is balanced in this regard. Jesus Himself teaches that the issue is not whether you judge, but how you judge. He also warns that the standard you use for judgment is the standard by which you yourself will be judged (Matthew 7:2).

So if you are judging others with evil intent, God will bring it back upon your own head. (I'm convinced that some of the things I see believers going through are the result of this principle being carried out in their lives.) God is very protective of His children. Even though some of His kids need to be corrected for the wrong they have done, the correction should always have the goal of restoring them to fellowship and building them up. We can do this effectively only when we have removed the log from our own eye, and that important surgery requires humility before God (Matthew 7:1-5).

Again, when you slander and pass wrong judgment, you set yourself up as judge, jury, and executioner. You are playing God. But there is only one God, the Bible says. "There is only one Lawgiver and Judge, the One who is able to save and to destroy; but who are you who judge your neighbor?" (James 4:12).

God is the only One able to render righteous judgment perfectly. If you position yourself as the final authority, you are setting yourself up for a big fall. That's why the Bible warns, "Let him who thinks he stands take heed that he does not fall" (1 Corinthians 10:12). This is clearly a call to humility. When we see someone caught up in sin, pride causes us to look down on that person and say, "That could never happen to me." But the humble person knows better: "But for the grace of God, that could be me." When you understand this, you can indeed humble yourself before God.

Jesus told a story about two men who went to the temple to pray. The Pharisee stood up proudly and said, "God, I thank You that I am not like other people" (Luke 18:11). As he went on to list various sinners, he noticed a tax collector standing next to him—a perfect example of the kind of sinner he was talking about. So the Pharisee thanked God that he was not like that low-life tax collector.

But the tax collector had a different attitude. He would not even approach the altar, but stood back, beat his chest in agony over his sins, and cried out, "God, be merciful to me, the sinner" (verse 13).

Jesus said the tax collector went away justified, while the Pharisee went away condemned. Why? Because the person who thinks he is high will be brought low, but the one who goes low will be lifted high.

That tax collector knew what it meant to pursue God. Despite his sins, despite his evil deeds, he wanted to draw close to God more than he wanted anything else. He also knew what God required if he were to draw near to Him: a humble awareness of his sin and need for God.

What about you? Do you have a desire for God that will not be satisfied with anything less than deep, personal intimacy with Him? Wherever you are in your spiritual life, you can decide to pursue God with greater intimacy. You can regroup like a football team at halftime.

At halftime, the teams stop playing and rally together. No matter what happened in the first half, they still have time to do something. The game isn't over yet.

Right now, it's only halftime in your spiritual life. You still have another half to get back out on the field and play to win. Don't listen to the crowd or to anyone else except Jesus Christ. He is calling you to intimate fellowship with Himself. It is time for your comeback!

Reflection and Application Questions

1. The final chapter in our study on your comeback focuses on pursuing a deeper level of intimacy with God. Tony offers three ways to approach intimacy: (1) Submit to God, (2) resist the devil, and (3) draw near to God. Take a moment to consider which one of these three ways gives you the biggest challenge in your life. Write down some things that get in the way of you

pursuing God more fully. These could be tangible, such as a busy schedule, or they could be intangible, such as worry or anxiety.

2. Tony's illustration of wheels on a car being out of alignment gives us insight into what happens in our lives when we are not aligned with God and His will, truth, and Word. List some possible negative consequences that come from being out of alignment with God.

   a. Is there a time in your life when you have experienced negative consequences because your choices were out of alignment with God? Write down a few things you could have done differently. How does this reshape your thinking about aligning yourself and submitting to God in all things?

   b. When a car's wheels are out of alignment, the tires suffer extra wear and tear. Similarly, as believers we experience excessive wear and tear on our lives when we operate outside of God's will. Spend a moment listing some positive outcomes for living life in alignment with God's Word.

3. According to James 4:7, what does Satan do when you resist him?

   a. In what ways can you "resist the devil" in your personal life?

   b. In what ways do you tend to open the door and give the devil an opportunity to twist your thinking and choices?

4. Tony compares cultivating intimacy with God and cultivating intimacy in a marriage. It takes time and intention to maintain an intimate relationship with anyone. How high on your priority list is cultivating intimacy with the Lord? How can you implement practical steps to move it even higher?

5. Based on the content in this book, take a moment to prayerfully construct a spiritual strategy to put you in the best position possible for your comeback. Then spend some time praying over this strategy. Review it as often as necessary until you feel you are implementing it fully.

CONCLUSION

The Patriots were down 25 points, with only a quarter and some change to go. Anyone putting their wager on New England coming back to win Super Bowl 51 (other than the Patriots, their fans, and their families) would have been laughed out of town.

There was no way they could win.

ESPN gave them less than a 1 percent win probability at that. No team comes back from a 25-point deficit to win the Super Bowl. Not on this stage. Not with this much at stake. That's four scores in roughly one quarter—including some two-point conversions—while simultaneously stopping an offense that has already put up 28 points.

There were two issues with this theory. First, the Patriots hadn't figured out how to score a touchdown against Atlanta's D-line yet. Second…multiple two-point conversions? They had only attempted two two-point conversions all season long, and they were successful on just one. To make multiple two-point conversions in this game…not likely.

As I said, few people believed this deficit could be overcome (outside of the Patriots and their fans and families). The Falcons were already licking their chops. Atlanta fans had begun celebrating and trying to determine which one of their players would be crowned Super Bowl MVP—would it be Matt Ryan, or how about Grady Jarret with three fierce sacks? Even the president of the United States left his own Super Bowl party in Palm Beach right after the Falcons went up 28-3.

On social media, Twitter unloaded with a heyday of Tom Brady "deflated" memes to add to the celebration. And when @The_Real_Fan tweeted to Fox Sports commentator Shannon Sharpe in the fourth quarter: "How impressive would it be if Pats make an historic 2nd Half comeback?" Sharpe had only this sharp reply: "Biggest comeback in SB history is 10 pts. Washington versus Broncos, Pats versus Seahawks" In other words, "Grow up. Ain't happening tonight."

Most of the 111 million people watching had come to the same conclusion: No one comes back from a 25-point deficit. Not even the "comeback king" Tom Brady himself.

On top of all this, the Patriots' defense would have to figure out a way to stop Matty Ice, the NFL's newly named MVP, at least four times as well.

It just wasn't going to happen.

Or was it?

Against all odds, the Patriots and their fans and families believed it would. Patriot receiver Julian Edelman was heard sharing shortly after the game, "There's a saying that me and Amendola say all of the time: You just gotta believe!"[1]

And believe they did.

Midway through the third quarter, the Patriots began a six-and-a-half-minute, thirteen-play drive that would include a conversion on fourth and three, as well as a Brady scramble for fifteen yards. Brady scramble? Yes, he did. The drive ended with a five-yard touchdown pass to running back James White and a failed attempt at an extra point. The score stood now at 28-9. ESPN kept them at the less than 1 percent win probability.

But next up was a seventy-two-yard, twelve-play drive that took more than five minutes off the clock. This one ended in a Brady sack just behind the ten-yard line and a thirty-three-yard field goal to make it 28-12. Still ESPN kept the win probability at less than 1 percent.

Maybe you remember where you were during this part of the game, and how the energy in the room began to shift as the Patriots kept coming back time after time after time. People started to sit up and pay attention. After all, having scored twice on two drives, the Patriots could conceivably tie the game with two touchdowns and two two-point conversions.

Possible? Maybe.

Likely? Not at all.

But a stripped ball led to a quick change of possession, a Brady pass into the end zone was followed by a two-point conversion, and the game was now 28-20.

By now, most people watching the game were in a state of disbelief. What seemed like a certain lock for Atlanta was now a one-score game. And a one-score game with Brady on the bottom usually meant a win for the Patriots.

But the Falcons had the ball, and if they could simply run out the clock and score, it would be a wrap. The Patriots didn't make that easy. In fact, the defense made another strong stop, giving the ball back to Brady with three minutes and thirty seconds still on the clock.

Starting from their own nine-yard line, the Patriots marched defiantly down the field, where Edelman made his "immaculate reception," cradling the ball in his hands just inches above the field while diving between three defenders. A couple more completed passes, a run for the score by James White, a two-point conversion by Amendola…and suddenly all of America sat in a stunned silence. Tie game.

A coin toss, six passes, and a few run plays later, James White punched it in again, this time for the greatest comeback win in Super Bowl history. And, aside from the Buffalo Bills in 1993, this is likely the greatest comeback in NFL history as well.

After the game, Brady had this to say about James White, the little-known player who scored three touchdowns and one two-point conversion on the way to their comeback: "He is everything you want in a player—dependable, consistent, durable."[2] Sounds like he's describing most players on the Patriots team, even himself. That's their culture. That's also why they come back so well.

Why have I've chosen to use this jaw-dropping comeback as the conclusion for our time together on this theme? Over and over, in reviews of the plays and interviews with the players and coaches, we heard about qualities and decisions that reflect what we must do if we are to experience our own comebacks in life—qualities like dependability, consistency, resilience, patience, preparation, wisdom, humility, faith, belief, and obedience. Each and every one of those qualities helped the Patriots win the Lombardi Trophy in Super Bowl 51. And you too will need them in turning your setback into a comeback.

It might help if we look a little more closely at how these qualities were applied. Faced with adverse circumstances, Brady stayed open to changing his plan. He threw the ball to parts of the field he doesn't typically go to, he involved every one of his teammates, and he made small moves to pick up yardage bit by bit. This type of football requires an enormous amount of patience and discipline from the all the offensive players—especially the quarterback. It doesn't make for quick scores from deep passes or long runs—the kind of plays we're so used to seeing in Super Bowls. And late in the game running out, it's counterintuitive to continue taking time off of the clock for such small gains.

But Brady's and the Patriots' patience and discipline gained them the respect of an entire nation (outside of Atlanta) in one night. Their willingness to work outside their comfort zone, adjust their strategy midstream, and stay calm in the midst of what looked like chaos were just as important as their athletic skills. They also picked apart the defense by consistently controlling the ball and eventually wearing them down.

These football skills are similar to the skills we have looked at together in this book. For your comeback, you will need wisdom, patience, guidance, resilience, adaptability, and surrender to the overall goal from above. Apply those skills to the setback you are facing, and you'll ultimately reach your comeback. It may not be in the way you had hoped or imagined. But when you finally do get there, it will be nothing short of amazing.

Naaman, Peter, Hannah, Gehazi, and Jehoshaphat all applied these skills in their own ways. Naaman wanted to go for the long ball and the glory plays, but he had to settle for seven dips in the Jordan River. His obedience brought him his comeback. Peter thought he knew the best game strategy on the sea. When Jesus told him to cast his nets on the other side, he could have argued and refused—sticking with what he knew best. But he didn't. He became adaptable to an adjustment in the approach. As a result, Peter experienced an amazing comeback after what had been a lousy night of fishing.

Hannah demonstrated great patience in going to the temple time and time again with her request. She also believed what the priest had told her, and she received the child she had longed for— plus more. Gehazi showed great humility in revealing that he had learned from his past mistakes. Humility allows us to acknowledge our mistakes and grow from them, rather than wallow in them— which gets us nowhere. Gehazi got his comeback as well. And then there's Jehoshaphat, who essentially said, like Julian Edelman, "You just gotta believe!" That belief keeps heads held high and positive praise on the lips of those facing a challenging setback.

Each of these biblical characters showed the qualities that make for a comeback. Keep in mind, comebacks don't happen just because you want them to happen. They happen because you prepare, study, discipline yourself, position yourself, and allow yourself to be adaptable to God's plan. Comebacks don't happen every day, but that's what makes them so special when they do.

Tom Brady said in his postgame interview, "This win came

from a lot of mental toughness by our team. That's why you play to the end. It's a 60-minute game. Because of it, this team will be mentioned with the great teams because of the way we finished it out."[3]

Friend, if you're still here, your game is not over either. It's not too late. Play to the end. Be mentally and spiritually tough. If you do, then one day you will be mentioned with the greats in heaven because of the way you finished it out.

Here's to your comeback. I look forward to hearing about it on high.

NOTES

Chapter 1: Think Different

1. Stuart Elliot, "I.B.M.'s multimedia campaign posits that small is beautiful," *New York Times*, August 28, 1997, http://www.nytimes.com/1997/08/28/business/ibm-s-multimedia-campaign-posits-that-small-is-beautiful.html.

2. Cited in Rob Stiltanen, "The Real Story Behind Apple's 'Think Different' Campaign," *Forbes*, December 14, 2011, http://www.forbes.com/sites/onmarketing/2011/12/14/the-real-story-behind-apples-think-different-campaign/.

3. Tom Schulman, *Dead Poet's Society*, directed by Peter Weir (Burbank, CA: Touchstone Pictures, 1989).

4. Kenneth Roman, "What Is the Best Advertising Campaign of All Time?" *Atlantic*, March 2015, http://www.theatlantic.com/magazine/archive/2015/03/the-big-question/384984/.

Chapter 2: Embrace the Unusual

1. Daniel J. Simons and Christopher F. Chabris, "Gorillas in our midst: Sustained inattentional blindness for dynamic events," *Perception* 28 (1999): 1059-74, http://www.chabris.com/Simons1999.pdf.

2. Ira E. Hyman, et al., "Did you see the unicycling clown? Inattentional blindness while walking and talking on a cell phone," *Applied Cognitive Psychology* 5 (2009): 597–607, http://onlinelibrary.wiley.com/doi/10.1002/acp.1638/abstract.

3. Denise Grady, "The Vision Thing: Mainly in the Brain," *Discover*, June 1, 1993, http://discovermagazine.com/1993/jun/thevisionthingma227.

4. Carolyn Thompson, "Bullied NY Bus Monitor Teaches Kindness Year Later," *USA Today*, June 25, 2013, https://www.usatoday.com/story/news/nation/2013/06/24/bullied-ny-bus-monitor/2451751/.

Chapter 3: Don't Stay Down

1. Dominique Mosbergen, "This Inspiring Runner Took a Nasty Fall, but She Didn't Stay Down for Long," *Huffington Post*, May 27, 2014, http://www.huffingtonpost.com/2014/05/27/runner-falls-wins-race-heather-dorniden_n_5395232.html.

2. Rick Moore, "Big Fish, Big Pond," cited in "Heather Dorniden: The Runner Who Didn't Give Up," *NHNE Pulse*, May 13, 2009, http://nhne-pulse.org/heather-dorniden-the-runner-who-didnt-give-up/.

3. Heather Kampf, "Monday in Minnesota—Tuesday, Poland" (Blog post), March 5, 2014, http://heatherkampf.blogspot.com.

4. Lee Moran, "Marine runs alongside boy struggling to finish 5k race," *New York Daily News*, August 2, 2013, http://www.nydailynews.com/news/national/marine-runs-boy-struggling -finish-5k-race-article-1.1415589.

5. Sasha Goldstein, "High school runner carries rival across finish line at North Dakota cross-country race," *New York Daily News*, October 17, 2014, http://www.nydailynews.com/sports/ high-school-runner-carries-rival-finish-line-cross-country-race-article-1.1978574.

Chapter 4: Keep Moving Forward

1. Taylor Pittman, "'Butterfly Child' With Rare, Painful Condition Displays Strength That Will Blow You Away," *Huffington Post*, April 25, 2015, http://www.huffingtonpost .com/2015/04/21/jonathan-pitre-the-butterfly-child_n_7108284.html.

2. Monica Lewinsky, "The Price of Shame," *TED*, March 2015, http://www.ted.com/talks/ monica_lewinsky_the_price_of_shame/transcript?language=en.

3. Ibid.

4. Ibid.

5. Domonique Bertolucci, "What Monica Lewinsky's Comeback Can Teach Us All," *News.com.au*, April 18, 2015, http://www.news.com.au/lifestyle/real-life/what-monica-lewinskys-comeback -can-teach-us-all/story-fnq2o7hp-1227309776946.

6. Jessica Bennett, "Monica Lewinsky Is Back, But This Time It's on Her Terms," *New York Times*, March 19, 2015, http://www.nytimes.com/2015/03/22/style/monica-lewinsky-is-back-but -this-time-its-on-her-terms.html.

Chapter 5: Stare Down the Challenge

1. John Dennen, "How Manny Pacquiao recovered from the knockout loss to Juan Manuel Marquez," *Boxing News*, November 22, 2014, http://www.boxingnewsonline.net/ how-manny-pacquiao-recovered-from-the-devastating-loss-to-juan-manuel-marquez/.

2. Martin Rogers, "Manny Pacquiao dominates Chris Algieri in unanimous decision," *USA Today*, November 23, 2014, http://www.usatoday.com/story/sports/boxing/2014/11/23/ manny-pacquiao-chris-algieri-macau-welterweight-title-fight/19434441/.

3. Kevin Mitchell, "Manny Pacquiao: 'I changed when I heard the voice of God,'" *The Guardian*, October 4, 2014, http://www.theguardian.com/sport/2014/oct/04/manny-pacquiao-chris -algieri-floyd-mayweather.

4. Ibid.

Conclusion

1. "Edelman Postgame Field Interview: 'It's an honor to get to play with a guy like Tom Brady'" (Video), *NFL World*, February 5, 2017, https://www.youtube.com/watch?v=WO_gkV62QrA.

2. "Tom Brady Post-Game Interview: That was 'exactly how we didn't plan it,'" *NFL World*, February 5, 2017, https://www.youtube.com/watch?v=puxt_xUTQxY.

3. "Tom Brady Post-Game Interview."

DR. TONY EVANS AND THE
URBAN ALTERNATIVE

About Dr. Tony Evans

Dr. Tony Evans is founder and senior pastor of the 10,000-member Oak Cliff Bible Fellowship in Dallas, founder and president of the Urban Alternative, chaplain of the NBA's Dallas Mavericks, and author of many books, including *Destiny* and *Victory in Spiritual Warfare*. His radio broadcast, *The Alternative with Dr. Tony Evans*, can be heard on more than 1,000 outlets and in more than 100 countries.

The Urban Alternative

The Urban Alternative (TUA) equips, empowers, and unites Christians to impact individuals, families, churches, and communities through a thoroughly kingdom agenda worldview. In teaching truth, we seek to transform lives.

The core cause of the problems we face in our personal lives, homes, churches, and societies is spiritual; therefore, the only way to address it is spiritually. We've tried a political, social, economic, and even a religious agenda. It's time for a kingdom agenda—the visible manifestation of the comprehensive rule of God over every area of life.

The unifying, central theme of the Bible is the glory of God and the advancement of His kingdom. This is the conjoining thread from Genesis to Revelation—from beginning to end. Without that theme, the Bible might look like disconnected stories that are inspiring but seem to be unrelated in purpose and direction. The Bible exists to share God's movement in history to establish and expand His kingdom, highlighting the connectivity throughout, which is the kingdom. Understanding that increases the relevance of these ancient writings in our day-to-day living because the kingdom is not only then—it is now.

The absence of the kingdom's influence in our own lives and in our families, churches, and communities has led to a catastrophic deterioration in our world.

- People live segmented, compartmentalized lives because they lack God's kingdom worldview.

- Families disintegrate because they exist for their own satisfaction rather than for the kingdom.

- Churches have limited impact because they fail to comprehend that the goal of the church is not to advance the church itself, but the kingdom.

- Communities have nowhere to turn to find real solutions for real people who have real problems, because the church has become divided, ingrown, and powerless to transform the cultural landscape in any relevant way.

The kingdom agenda offers us a way to live with a solid hope by optimizing the solutions of heaven. When God and His rule are not the final and authoritative standard over all, order and hope are lost. But the reverse of that is true as well—as long as we have God, we have hope. If God is still in the picture, and as long as His agenda is still on the table, it's not over.

Even if relationships collapse, God will sustain you. Even if finances dwindle, God will keep you. Even if dreams die, God will revive you. As long as God and His rule guide your life, family, church, and community, there is always hope.

Our world needs the King's agenda. Our churches need the King's agenda. Our families need the King's agenda.

In many major cities, drivers can take a loop to get to the other side of the city without driving straight through downtown. This loop takes them close enough to the city to see its towering buildings and skyline, but not close enough to actually experience it.

This is precisely what our culture has done with God. We have put Him on the "loop" of our personal, family, church, and community lives. He's close enough to be at hand should we need Him in an emergency, but far enough away that He can't be the center of who we are.

Sadly, we often want God on the loop of our lives, but we don't always want the King of the Bible to come downtown into the very heart of our ways. Leaving God on the loop brings about dire consequences, as we have seen in our own lives and with others. But when we make God and His rule the centerpiece of all we think, do, and say, we experience Him in the way He longs for us to.

He wants us to be kingdom people with kingdom minds set on fulfilling His kingdom purposes. He wants us to pray as Jesus did—"Not my will, but Yours be done" (Luke 22:42)—because His is the kingdom, the power, and the glory.

There is only one God, and we are not Him. As King and Creator, God calls the shots. Only when we align ourselves underneath His comprehensive authority will we access His full power and authority in our lives, families, churches, and communities.

As we learn how to govern ourselves under God, we will transform the institutions of family, church, and society according to a biblically based, kingdom worldview. Under Him, we touch heaven and change earth.

To achieve our goal, we use a variety of strategies, approaches, and resources for reaching and equipping as many people as possible.

Broadcast Media

Millions of individuals experience *The Alternative with Dr. Tony Evans*, a daily broadcast playing on nearly 1,000 radio outlets and in more than 100 countries. The broadcast can also be seen on several television networks, online at TonyEvans.org, and on the free Tony Evans app. More than four million message downloads occur each year.

Leadership Training

The *Tony Evans Training Center (TETC)* facilitates educational programming that embodies the ministry philosophy of Dr. Tony Evans as expressed through the kingdom agenda. The training courses focus on leadership development and discipleship in five tracks:

- Bible and theology
- personal growth
- family and relationships
- church health and leadership development
- society and community impact

The TETC program includes courses for both local and online students. Furthermore, TETC programming includes course work for nonstudent attendees. Pastors, Christian leaders, and Christian laity, both local and at a distance, can seek the Kingdom Agenda Certificate for personal, spiritual, and professional development. Some courses qualify for continuing education credits and will transfer for college credit with our partner schools.

Kingdom Agenda Pastors (KAP) provides a viable network for like-minded pastors who embrace the kingdom agenda philosophy. Pastors have the opportunity to go deeper with Dr. Tony Evans as they are given greater biblical knowledge, practical applications, and resources to impact individuals, families, churches, and communities. KAP welcomes senior and associate pastors of all churches. KAP also offers an annual summit, held each year in Dallas, Texas, with intensive seminars, workshops, and resources.

Pastors' Wives Ministry, founded by Dr. Lois Evans, provides counsel, encouragement, and spiritual resources for pastors' wives as they serve with their husbands in ministry. A primary focus of the ministry is the KAP Summit, which offers senior pastors' wives a safe place to reflect, renew, and relax along with training in personal development, spiritual growth, and care for their emotional and physical well-being.

Community Impact

National Church Adopt-A-School Initiative (NCAASI) empowers churches across the country to impact communities through public schools, effecting positive social change in urban youth and families. Leaders of churches, school districts, faith-based organizations, and other nonprofit organizations are equipped with the knowledge and tools to forge partnerships and build strong social service delivery systems. This training is based on the comprehensive church-based community impact strategy conducted by Oak Cliff Bible Fellowship. It addresses areas such as economic development, education, housing, health revitalization, family renewal, and racial reconciliation. We assist churches in tailoring the model to meet specific needs of their communities, while addressing the spiritual and moral frame of reference. Training events are held annually in the Dallas area at Oak Cliff Bible Fellowship.

Athlete's Impact (AI) is as an outreach into and through sports. Coaches are sometimes the most influential adults in young people's lives—even more than parents. With the rise of fatherlessness in our culture, more young people are looking to their coaches for guidance, character development, practical needs, and hope. Athletes (professional or amateur) also influence younger athletes and kids. Knowing this, we equip and train coaches and athletes to live out and utilize their God-given roles for the benefit of the kingdom. We aim to do this through our iCoach App, weCoach Football Conference, and other resources, such as *The Playbook: A Life Strategy Guide for Athletes.*

Resource Development

We foster lifelong learning partnerships with the people we

serve by providing a variety of published materials. Dr. Evans has published more than 100 unique titles (booklets, books, and Bible studies) based on more than 40 years of preaching. Our goal is to strengthen individuals in their walk with God and service to others.

For more information
and a complimentary copy of
Dr. Evans's devotional newsletter,

call
(800) 800-3222

or write
TUA
PO Box 4000
Dallas TX 75208

or visit our website
www.TonyEvans.org

CONTINUE YOUR COMEBACK WITH...

Your Comeback DVD

Your Comeback Interactive Workbook

MORE GREAT HARVEST HOUSE BOOKS BY DR. TONY EVANS

30 Days to Overcoming Addictive Behavior

30 Days to Overcoming Emotional Strongholds

30 Days to Victory Through Forgiveness

Discover Your Destiny

Experience the Power of God's Names

Horizontal Jesus

Horizontal Jesus Study Guide

It's Not Too Late

A Moment for Your Soul (eBook only)

The Power of God's Names

Prayers for Victory in Spiritual Warfare

Prayers for Victory in Your Marriage

Praying Through the Names of God

Victory in Spiritual Warfare

Watch Your Mouth

Watch Your Mouth DVD

Watch Your Mouth Growth and Study Guide

Watch Your Mouth Interactive Workbook